365

activities
you and your baby
will love

GYMBOREE® PLAY & MUSIC

365

activities

you and your baby will love

author
susan elisabeth davis

consulting editors
dr. roni cohen leiderman & dr. wendy masi

illustrator
christine coirault

photographer
aaron locke

GYMBOREE [PLaY & MUSiC]

Produced by Weldon Owen Inc.,
814 Montgomery Street, San Francisco, California 94133,
in collaboration with the Gymboree Corporation, Inc.,
500 Howard Street, San Francisco, California 94105

Gymboree Play & Music Programs

Chief Executive Officer **Lisa Harper**
Product Manager **Lisa Biasotti**
Play & Music Senior Program Developer
Helene Silver Freda

Weldon Owen Inc.

Chief Executive Officer **John Owen**
Chief Operating Officer & President **Terry Newell**
Chief Financial Officer **Christine E. Munson**
Vice President & Publisher **Roger Shaw**
Vice President, International Sales **Stuart Laurence**

Publisher **Rebecca Poole Forée**
Managing Editor **Jennifer Block Martin**
Project Editor **Maria Behan**
Contributing Editors **Elizabeth Dougherty,
Margaret Sabo Wills**
Copy Editor **Gail Nelson-Bonebrake**
Proofreaders **Peter Cieply, David Sweet**
Indexer **Ken DellaPenta**
Editorial Assistant **Lucie Parker**

Creative Director **Gaye Allen**
Art Director **Lisa Milestone**
Production Director **Chris Hemesath**
Production Assistant **Meghan Hildebrand**

Library of Congress Control Number: 2005932888
ISBN 1-892374-66-8

Printed in China.

a special note on safety

At Gymboree, we encourage parents to become active play partners with their children. As you enjoy these enriching activities with your baby, make safety your priority. While the risk of injury during any of these activities is low, take every precaution to ensure that your child is safe.

To reduce the risk of injury, please follow these guidelines: do not leave your child unattended, even for a brief moment, during any of the activities in this book; be particularly cautious when participating in the activities involving water because of the risk of drowning; ensure that your baby does not place in his or her mouth any small objects (even those depicted in the photographs and illustrations), as some may pose a choking hazard and could be fatal if ingested; make sure that writing and crafts materials are nontoxic and have been approved for use by children under three years of age.

Throughout this book, we have suggested guidelines to the age appropriateness of each activity; however, it is up to you to assess your own child's suitability for a particular activity before attempting it. Ability, balance, and dexterity vary considerably from child to child, even for children of the same age.

While we have made every effort to ensure that the information is accurate and reliable, and that the activities are safe and workable when an adult is properly supervising, we disclaim all liability for any unintended, unforeseen, or improper application of the recommendations and suggestions featured in this book.

contents

birth
& up

1

three
months & up

88

six
months & up

173

nine
months & up

267

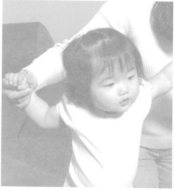

Foreword

Tummy tickles, peekaboo games, silly songs, and bubble blowing: the many ways parents use play to connect with their infants are endless. Play is universal—and it's the natural way to interact with your baby. But play is much more than just fun and games. It's how babies learn about themselves, others, and everything around them.

Gymboree's *365 Activities You and Your Baby Will Love* provides you with an idea for each day of your newborn's pivotal first year. These play activities are designed not only to entertain your infant, but also to help him or her learn about the world, hone physical and mental skills, and grow closer to you. Many of the activities originated from Gymboree's ever-popular Play & Music Programs. And to mirror your baby's major developmental milestones, the activities are divided into three-month age ranges, starting at birth and ending at 12 months.

Delight in your newborn's first year. The 365 days ahead are a journey that will bring more joy, fun, and fulfillment than you can imagine. Each day brings you opportunities to discover activities your baby will love and learn from—and we hope this book will be a great source of inspiration.

Dr. Roni Cohen Leiderman

Dr. Wendy Masi

0+

from birth & up

Newborns are fascinating creatures—their senses are developing, they're highly attuned to you, and they're engaged in their very first experiences of the world. At this age, play has more to do with comfort, bonding, and trust than it does with lively interactive activities. You can help your baby develop her muscles and sensory abilities at this stage, too. Just take it slow, and give her plenty of breaks to ensure that she doesn't get overstimulated.

1

soothe with heartbeats

Studies show that newborns are soothed by the sound of a human heartbeat, which they grew accustomed to hearing in the womb. Let your baby experience this comforting sound often by lying with him on your chest, skin to skin. Or sit in a chair and let his head rest against the left side of your chest, which psychologist Lee Salk and others have noted is the side on which most mothers intuitively hold their babies anyway. Notice how the sound and feel of your beating heart can calm your newborn.

2

talk often

Your baby is keenly attuned to the sound of your voice and to your facial expressions—she needs to be exposed to both to learn how to talk. Speak gently to soothe her, or talk quickly in an upbeat tone and with a range of facial expressions to make her eyes widen and her little head bobble with excitement.

3

revel in his reflection

Babies are very aware of faces, especially those of other babies. Let your baby indulge in this fascination by gazing at himself in the mirror for a while. He won't know who's looking back at him until he is about 12 to 15 months old, but he's bound to like what he sees.

4

take cues from your baby

The watchful eyes of a young baby are truly enchanting, in part because they are such obvious signs of intelligent, responsive life. But young babies are only alert for a half hour or so at a time and easily become overstimulated when presented with too much activity.

How can you tell if she's had enough? Make sure you tune into the cues your baby's giving you. She may turn her head away, start to cry, or become sleepy. Respecting her need for space or for interaction will give her a chance to control how much stimulation she's taking in. As a result, she'll feel confident about her place in—and effect on—the world.

5

lie under the trees

Together you and your newborn can watch the dance of light and shadow, feel the breeze upon your skin, and listen to the gentle *shhh shhh* of rustling leaves.

6

take a walk

A walk in the great outdoors will quiet—and fascinate—most babies, whether they're riding in a stroller or nestled close to your chest. And fresh air can do wonders for new parents, too.

7

tantalize with texture

Stroke large swatches of textured cloth like velvet, fake fur, corduroy, or satin across your baby's body. As his grasping ability develops, he'll start to hold the swatches himself and rub them between his fingers. (Make sure the swatches are at least 6 x 6 inches, or 15 x 15 cm, so they won't pose a choking hazard.) At around six months, he may even choose one to provide him comfort as he falls asleep at night.

8

rise and shine

Greet your baby in the morning with this
much-loved poem by Robert Louis Stevenson.

A birdie with a yellow bill
Hopped upon my window sill.
Cocked his shining eye and said,
"Get up, get up, you sleepyhead!"

9

look out the window

Give your baby time to gaze out a window.
The gentle sway of the curtains in the breeze, the
flickering shadows, and the sights and sounds of
passing birds will entrance her, as well as stimulate
her vision and sharpen her ability to locate noises
coming from different directions.

10

dress alike

From the moment you bring your baby home, well-meaning observers will tell you how to dress your child. Often the recommendation will be to put more clothing on him. However, too much clothing can result in dangerous overheating. While newborns need to be kept warm because they can't regulate their own temperature, after the first month, a baby's body is able to conserve heat.

Here's a good rule of thumb: For newborns, put on one more layer of clothing than what you're wearing. After the first month, your baby doesn't need to wear any more or less clothing than you do (unless you've built up a sweat from exercise or another activity).

11

"look me in the eyes...
Eye contact makes me feel
attached and teaches me
how to talk without words.**"**

12

play familiar tunes

Newborns perk up to music they heard in the womb—whether it was Bach, U2, or big sister's warbling rendition of "Rock-a-Bye Baby." Playing familiar music will stimulate your baby's mind and help her feel like her new world is safe and interesting.

13

make funny noises

Your baby loves to hear you talk and laugh. You can help stimulate his auditory development—and get a good giggle going—by making all sorts of funny noises. Try squawking like a parrot, honking like a truck horn, or saying "hello, hello, hello!" in a squeaky voice. He'll be amused—and amazed—and someday will surprise you by initiating silly sounds himself.

14

trace the tootsies

This light tickle game teaches about body parts.

Round and round the baby's feet
trace your fingers around your baby's feet

The birdie says, "Tweet, tweet, tweet! "
tap your fingers on her feet

Round and round the baby's head
trace your fingers around her head

Now the birdie says, "It's time for bed!"
kiss her forehead

15

tickle, tickle, tickle

Tickling your newborn with a clean feather duster helps him feel where his body begins and ends. Keep "dusting" your baby, and by about three months of age he's likely to giggle every time you pull out that "toy."

16

stretch out

Stretching your newborn's arms and legs helps her uncurl from her fetal position and become aware of her limbs. Gently pull her arms above her head, one at a time, and then slowly pull her legs down, one at a time, until they're almost straight. Be sure to stop if your baby isn't enjoying the stretches.

17

pat baby's back

When your baby is fussy, sleepy, or just needing a little physical contact, pat him gently on his back. This action helps him dispel gas, distracts him from too much stimulation in his environment, and simply reassures him that you're there.

18

wear your wee one

You'll quickly realize that your baby's favorite place to be is right against your chest. Many babies, in fact, start fussing as soon as they are set down. Your infant's need for physical contact—and rhythmic motion—is natural; instinct tells her that she needs to be near someone to be safe. Satisfy her desire for contact by "wearing" her, in either a sling or a front carrier. An oft-cited study of mother-infant pairs found that six-week-old babies who were "worn" for at least three hours a day cried only half as much as those babies who were not. Carrying your infant also helps her develop the muscles required to sit, stand, and walk, because she is in a semi-upright or upright position, which naturally strengthens her neck and back muscles.

19

flatter him

When your baby tries to imitate you, it shows
that you're his first and most important teacher. So
imagine how flattered he'll feel when you imitate
his gentle coos, his sweet "ahhhhs," and his quirky,
crooked smiles. It's a wonderful way to make
him feel that he's someone special.

20

start cycling lessons

Moving your baby's legs in a cycling motion helps her
develop awareness of her tiny body. It also strengthens
her abdominal muscles and introduces her to the idea
of alternating motion (one leg, then the other) that
she'll need to master in order to crawl. You'll enjoy the
face-to-face time that this activity allows, too.

21

sing a sweet lullaby

When your baby fusses, sing the time-honored
lullaby "Hush, Little Baby" to relax him.

Hush, little baby, don't say a word,
Papa's gonna buy you a mockingbird

And if that mockingbird won't sing,
Papa's gonna buy you a diamond ring

And if that diamond ring turns brass,
Papa's gonna buy you a looking glass

And if that looking glass gets broke,
Papa's gonna buy you a billy goat

And if that billy goat won't pull,
Papa's gonna buy you a cart and bull

And if that cart and bull fall down,
You'll still be the sweetest little baby in town.

22

dance to the beat

Dancing with babies is an age-old technique for helping them fall asleep or settle down. It provides them with the swaying motion and physical contact that they crave.

Some babies enjoy lullabies; others prefer rock'n'roll. Whatever your baby's preference, swaying with her held in your arms is a great way to bond, and it does wonders to both calm a child and ease a stressed parent's soul. In years to come, hearing the music that you and your baby danced to will bring back tender memories.

23

"let me play on a blanket...
When I lie on my tummy, I can stretch out my arms and legs, lift my head, and wave my hands.**"**

24

soar like an airplane

Hold your baby beneath his tummy with his
face looking downward. For many infants, this
position is particularly soothing when they're
gassy or very tired. Gently move him up and
down for a soothing and fun "airplane" ride.

25

make diaper changes playful

The chore of changing diapers can also be a playful
ritual. Give your baby a clean diaper to hold, and take it
back with a cheery "thank you." Then sing "up goes the
bottom" and "on goes the diaper" as you change her.
Just as a bedtime routine can help coax her to sleep, a
well-honed diaper routine can encourage cooperation.

26

smack your lips

Soft lip-smacking sounds soothe many jangled babies. The late anthropologist Ashley Montagu wrote in his book *Touching: The Human Significance of the Skin,* "The infant identifies the sounds and the lips from which they emerge with pleasurable experiences," such as being kissed.

27

play with paper plates

Use your baby's attraction to faces to help him learn how to track objects visually—that is, to move his eyes and head together to follow objects. Draw a simple smiling face on a paper plate or a round piece of paper. Holding the drawing 8 to 15 inches (20 to 38 cm) in front of his face, slowly move it from side to side.

28

make contact

Young babies thrive on the warmth of another human. One Swedish study showed that newborns who were given skin-to-skin contact with their mothers cried far less than those who were not. A recent South African report also found that babies given skin-to-skin contact stayed warmer and breathed easier than those who spent their first days in incubators. Even beyond the newborn stage, contact between baby and parent provides deep emotional and physical comfort.

29

follow the fish

Set your child in front of a fish tank in a pet store, at an aquarium, or at home. Watching the fish dart this way and that will amuse her and help her learn to track objects with her eyes.

30

blow gently

Lightly blowing on your baby's skin heightens his sense of touch. Blow on his fingers, tummy, and toes while changing his diaper. It might provide a helpful distraction if he gets impatient during the process—and it might even inspire a smile.

31

listen to wind chimes

Hearing is the first sense that develops fully in a newborn (even fetuses can hear while in the womb). Wind chimes stimulate hearing (not to mention the sense of seeing), and your baby will love listening to the tinkling sounds, while watching the dangling pieces sway in the breeze.

32

satisfy by smiling

Smile often at your baby. This simple act makes her feel special and shows her she's loved. When she learns to smile back, you'll feel loved, too.

33

blow on a pinwheel

The whirring movement and flashing colors of a pinwheel mesmerize even very young babies—and at about three months of age, they might try to grab the spinning wheel. To give your baby the best view, hold the pinwheel about two feet (60 cm) from his face and blow on it. Don't let him hold it, though, as the edges of a pinwheel could be sharp.

34

snuggle and sway

Cradle an unsettled baby upright chest-to-chest to soothe her with enclosing full-body contact. Gently rock or sway, while the baby looks out over your shoulder. Or snuggle her up under your chin where she'll feel gentle vibrations as you talk or hum.

35

encourage daydreaming

With all the emphasis on actively engaging babies, keep in mind that they are sometimes content to simply daydream, just like grown-ups. If your baby is gazing at his mobile or practicing lifting and lowering his tiny hand, let him enjoy the quiet time. He's not only learning to entertain himself, he's also increasing his ability to concentrate.

36

read to your infant

While your newborn won't understand the stories you read to her, she will love being nestled in your arms and listening to the rise and fall of your voice. And studies show that because babies who are read to during infancy hear more words, they typically develop a larger vocabulary when they are older.

37

say his name often

Your newborn has no concept of who he is, or even that he's a separate being with his own name. Tell him his name often—and with tenderness in your voice. It will help him learn that he's both loved and unique.

38

lull with a lullaby

Singing to your baby as she drifts off to sleep is a time-tested and cherished ritual. Here's a soothing version of Brahms' lullaby to add to your bedtime repertoire.

Lullaby and good night,
in the sky stars are bright.
Round your head, flowers gay,
bring you slumbers today.
Go to sleep now and rest,
may these hours be blessed.
Go to sleep now and rest,
may these hours be blessed.

39

blink your eyes

Stare directly at your baby and blink your eyes rapidly. It might just make him smile—and may give your little imitator something new to try.

40

massage your newborn

The pressure and motion of a gentle massage help young babies' immature digestive and circulatory systems develop. At a time when you're relaxed and your baby is receptive, remove her clothes. Rub an unscented, natural, edible oil like almond, grapeseed, or olive between your hands. Gently touch and knead her arms, legs, back, and tummy. (Avoid products with mineral oil, which can leave a greasy film and block pores, and peanut oil, in case your baby is allergic.)

41

"make faces at me...
Since I was just hours old,
I've imitated your facial
expressions, from big smiles
to wide-eyed surprise."

42

hold fingers

Your infant's grasp reflex makes him curl his
tiny fingers around your finger when you stroke
his palm. While this response is pure reflex, letting
your baby hold your fingers promotes attachment
and introduces him to the pleasure of touch.

43

dangle the ribbons

Indulge your baby's growing interest in movement
and color. Tie several short ribbons about 6 inches
(15 cm) long onto a bracelet or plastic clothes hanger.
Flutter the ribbons in front of her, letting them tickle
her arms and legs. As she grows older, she'll reach
out to touch the captivating ribbons.

44

name that part

After a bath, teach your baby the names of body parts by gently running a soft terry-cloth towel all over his body, naming each stop on the tour.

45

smell the roses

Your baby was born with an extremely refined sense of smell. Immediately after birth, babies can even recognize the smell of their mothers. Indeed, one way newborns find their mother's nipple is through scent.

Stimulate your infant's sense of smell by passing pleasantly scented objects, such as flowers, oranges, or vanilla extract, beneath her nose. She can't sniff voluntarily (that doesn't happen until about 18 months of age), but she'll enjoy smelling sweet scents in the air.

46

cruise in your car

Many fussy babies calm down and even fall asleep
when they're driven around in a car. Sometimes that
effect kicks in after 5 minutes; sometimes it takes
15 minutes or more. See if your baby is soothed into
slumber by a car ride—and have an audiobook or CD
handy to keep yourself entertained along the way.

47

travel with toys

On some days, a tote bag full of goodies may be the
one thing that will keep your baby (and you!) from
having meltdowns in the car. Stock rattles, board
books, and toys, and change the bag's contents often
so you'll always have a new diversion readily at hand.

48

put it in black and white

Your newborn can see the high contrast of simple large black-and-white patterns more easily than the subtle shades of brightly colored ones. To help stimulate his vision, hang black-and-white images—a mobile or framed fabric, for example—where he can see them. By about two months of age, your baby will be able to distinguish the subtle shades of gray almost as well as you can.

49

swing together

The peaceful swaying of a hammock relaxes babies and stimulates their vestibular system, the body's mechanism for maintaining balance and sensing movement through space. If your hammock is woven out of rope, cover it with a thick towel to make your baby's head and back more comfortable and to keep her hands and feet safely out of the webbing. Don't leave your baby alone or fall asleep with her in the hammock, however, because if she rolls into you she may not be able to lift her head to breathe.

50

shake the rattles

Once your baby has demonstrated an ability to grasp things, he'll enjoy holding and shaking light rattles. His first rattle-shaking will be involuntary. But hearing the rattling sound will help him eventually learn that cause (moving the toy) creates effect (noise). Start with light plastic or cloth rattles; heavy rattles are too difficult for young babies to hold, and they can hit themselves in the head with them.

51

sing a scrub-a-dub song

Sing this simple ditty to the tune of "Frère Jacques"
to entertain your baby during bath time.

Now we're washing
Now we're washing
Baby's toes
Baby's toes.
Now we're washing knees and
Now we're washing elbows
And baby's nose
And baby's nose.

52

bathe with baby

Taking a bath together is one of life's great
pleasures—for baby and parent alike. Cradle
your baby in your arms, play little splashing
games, and experiment with textured cloths
and sponges. The water should be warm but
not hot. Before you get out of the tub, hand
your baby to another grown-up or place her
on a thick towel near the tub (never stand
up with a wet, slippery baby in your hands).

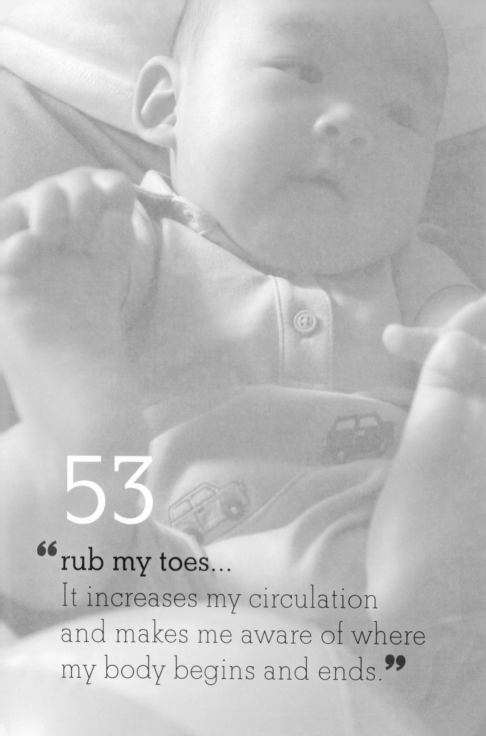

53

"rub my toes...
It increases my circulation
and makes me aware of where
my body begins and ends."

54

tease the "piggies"

This traditional game will delight your child.

This little piggy went to market
gently tug a different toe with each line

This little piggy stayed home

This little piggy had roast beef

This little piggy had none

And this little piggy cried

"Whee, whee, whee!" all the way home.
tickle his tummy with "Whee, whee, whee!"

55

play peekaboo

Look at your baby. Now look away. Look at him again,
then look away. Sneak another peek—and look away.
Now listen! He'll call you back with gurgles and coos.

56

build some bedtime routines

In the big, surprising world, babies love the security of rituals and repetition, especially when it's time to go to sleep. As you and your baby develop a bedtime routine, include activities that your baby finds absorbing but not too exciting. Practical preparations might include a warm relaxing bath or spot-cleaning, followed by putting on fresh pajamas. It's never too early to start a bedtime reading habit, as a couple of short books can help lull a child to sleep.

Then move on to soft music, a soothing lullaby, a feeding, or a comforting cuddle in the rocking chair. Consider starting a custom of talking about the day's events—the conversation won't be one-sided for long. Once your child settles into a routine, it can provide continuity at bedtime for months, even years, to come.

57

mesmerize with a mobile

By about two months of age, babies are intrigued by musical mobiles. With their swirling, colorful objects and soothing melodies, these toys stimulate both vision and hearing. Entertain your infant by hanging a mobile above her crib or changing table. To ensure that your baby never gets caught up in the mobile's strings, keep it at least an adult arm's length away.

58

sing with the spider

While he won't be able to mimic your hand motions until he's about a year old, your baby will love listening to the travails of "The Itsy-Bitsy Spider." Add tactile stimulation by crawling the spider up his tummy, "pouring" the rain down his shoulders, and crossing his arms above his head to make the sun come out.

The itsy-bitsy spider went up the water spout,
"walk" your fingers up in the air

Down came the rain and washed the spider out.
wiggle your fingers downward to make rain

Out came the sun and dried up all the rain,
form a circle with your hands above your head

And the itsy-bitsy spider went up the spout again.
"walk" your fingers up again

59

play with shadows

Because babies are intrigued by moving objects as
well as by light and dark patterns, shadows tend
to fascinate them, too. In a darkened room, shine
a flashlight on your baby's mobile or wiggle your
fingers in front of a lamp to cast shadows on a wall.
Watch as her eyes widen and her feet kick with glee.

60

mix things up

Babies lose interest when shown the same thing
too often. So occasionally hang new pictures near
the crib, introduce a new rattle, or find a plush toy
that has a different squeak. Slightly changing your
baby's environment once in a while will help
heighten his awareness of his surroundings.

61

rock the night away

Never underestimate the calming properties of the time-honored rocking chair. Together, you and your baby can rock away the stresses of a stimulating day. Your baby will hear your voice, feel your warmth, and perhaps even drowse on your shoulder. She'll also begin to feel rhythm from the steady rocking of the chair, and understanding rhythm is essential to learning language.

62

come when he calls

Responding to your baby's cries teaches him that he has some control over his world, that people love him, and that it's safe to trust those who care for him. Don't worry, you can't spoil a young baby. You can only assure him that his wants and needs matter.

63

bounce for fun

An infant will enjoy a gentle bouncing ride on
your knee, as long as she can hold her own head
up, while you carefully support her. (Just be sure
you don't jiggle her too hard.) Add this jingle
sung to the tune of "Mary Had a Little Lamb"
to your knee ride for even more fun.

Oh, baby's on my knee, knee, knee
knee, knee, knee
knee, knee, knee
Baby's on my knee, knee, knee
And jiggling up and down.
bounce her lightly on your knee

Oh, baby's going whee, whee, whee
whee, whee, whee
whee, whee, whee
Baby's going whee, whee, whee
And now she's dipping down.
hold her to your chest and dip her slowly
backward, while supporting her head

64

"kiss my tummy...
It tickles, it makes me
smile, and it teaches
me where my tummy is."

65

pick the right moments

Babies are alert only for short periods of time. When your infant is calm and attuned to his surroundings, he'll be most likely to respond. Use these moments to introduce him to new toys, books, and music.

66

do baby sit-ups

The infant version of this exercise will help strengthen your child's neck muscles. Simply lay her on her back on a blanket and sit at her feet, facing her. Then firmly grasp the top corners of the blanket with both hands so it fits securely around her head and upper body like a sling. Gently pull her toward you, then gently lower her. Slowly repeat several times—until she indicates she's tired by looking away or squirming.

67

look sideways

At this age, your baby will tend to lie with his head to one side. Give him something to gaze at by placing colorful toys or simple drawings in the area where he looks. (If you use string to hang an item, make sure it's at least an adult arm's length away from the crib so it does not pose a strangulation hazard.)

68

dangle the toys

At around two months of age, your baby will start reaching for objects around her. Encourage her by holding a plush toy, a rattle, or plastic measuring spoons in front of her. Don't, however, hand an object to her too quickly or yank it out of her reach. To feel successful, she needs to aim for the toy and grasp it.

69

be part of the family

It's almost impossible to spend all of your waking hours interacting with your baby. But you can socialize with him while getting other things done by keeping him in a fairly well-trafficked area of your home. Safely tuck your baby in a stroller or bassinet and let him watch family members as they go about their business in the kitchen or living room. He can also hear them as they pass by, which will help him feel like he's part of the action.

70

get out and about

Beat cabin fever by taking short daily trips together. You can take your baby just about anywhere—to the market, a park, or the mall. New sights are stimulating and will introduce her to a variety of social situations.

71

stroke his hands

Help your baby become more aware of the
way his hands open and close. When his fists are
tightly clenched, stroke the back of each one, an
action that generally makes a baby relax his grip.

72

change her perspective

Offer your infant a new view and strengthen her body
at the same time by propping her on her side with
rolled-up blankets or turning her over onto her tummy.
Be attuned to signs that she's uninterested or tired—for
example, if she fusses or cries. And remember, when
it's time for her to sleep, lay her on her back.

73

create a baby journal

Maybe you feel you'll never forget her first fleeting smile or first bit of "ba-ba-ba" babbling. But today's memories will get crowded out by new events, as your baby keeps you in the present moment. So jot down a few notes each week documenting the discoveries and wonders of early babyhood. Keep the journal convenient, perhaps at bedside, or in your diaper-bag to use during that rare free moment in a waiting room.

Help your baby contribute some footprints or handprints, maybe even a series at three-month intervals. Use a nontoxic, washable, medium-dark stamp pad, found among scrapbooking supplies. For a clear print, bring first the pad and then the paper firmly to the wiggly foot. Someday, when your child sees these artworks, he won't believe he was ever that small (and you won't either).

74

soothe with song

She's too young to ask for a pony, but you can still please her with this melodic lullaby, "All the Pretty Little Horses."

Hush-a-bye, don't you cry,
go to sleepy, little baby.
When you wake, you'll have
all the pretty little horses.

Black and bay, dapple and gray,
coach and six little horses.
Hush-a-bye, don't you cry,
go to sleepy, little baby.

♡ ✗ ✗ ✗

75

admire sweet baby faces

British researchers recently found that babies, even newborns, are more attracted to designs that look like faces than any other designs. Babies examine faces with great care and as a result learn about the social cues inherent in various facial expressions. Show your baby the faces in this book and others. Which ones make him smile? Which ones puzzle him?

76

greet her with joy

Your baby learns about human emotions—including happiness, sadness, and the exhilaration of seeing a loved one—primarily from her family. Show her how people greet each other by giving her a big smile and a cheerful hello—and do it often throughout the day. By watching you, she'll learn and soon imitate what you do.

77

practice patience

Newborns need time to figure out how to do what they want to do—whether it's reaching out to grasp something, kicking at a toy, or imitating your facial expressions. Be patient during these fertile moments. If you rush to help your baby or turn away before he's done what he's trying to do, he'll get discouraged.

78

stick out your tongue

Babies are born knowing how to imitate many of the expressions they see on other faces. So try sticking out your tongue and see if your baby responds in kind. Or open your mouth wide and say "ahhhh" several times; she may open her mouth and say "ahhhh" right back.

79

bedeck him with bracelet bells

Help your baby understand that he has his own hands and assist him in getting used to how they move by putting a small colorful rattle-bracelet on his tiny wrist. Check that rattles, bells, and beads are securely attached to the bracelet to ensure that they never loosen and get into his mouth.

80

hug for happiness

Numerous studies have shown that holding a baby
releases the calming hormone oxytocin (also called
the "cuddle hormone") in both parent and child.
Hold her often: it will help calm you and your
baby, as well as promote greater attachment.

81

dress with success

It can be difficult—and distressing—to dress an infant
who's protesting: flopping his neck, flailing his arms,
maybe even wailing. Try singing or playing peekaboo
to distract him from the task at hand. If he doesn't like
being naked, cover him with a light blanket. Choose
easy-to-handle clothing, like tops with wide neckholes,
pajamas with zippers, and pants with elastic waists.

82

"lay me on a big beach ball...
Gently roll me back and forth
while holding me on top of the
ball, and I'll develop balance
and stronger neck muscles."

83

set up a floor gym

Even if your infant is too young to swat at the dangling toys of a floor gym, you can still lay her beneath one so she can look up at it. She will want to touch the appealing colors and shapes so much that someday soon she'll lift an arm and start batting away.

84

offer toys one at a time

As tempting as it is to give your child all of the toys, rattles, and playthings you've collected for him, hold yourself back. Since he can only hold one object at a time right now, having too much in his visual field may confuse or frustrate him. Give him one or two toys, and replace them when he appears bored. This will also help him focus—and prevent overstimulation.

85

make eye contact

Newborn babies can only focus on objects within 8 to 15 inches (20 to 38 cm) of their nose—the perfect distance for seeing a nursing mom's face. But your baby isn't able to track an object that moves from one side to the other. (In fact, she doesn't even know that moving her head along with her eyes expands her view.) To help strengthen her eye muscles so they can work together, slowly move brightly colored objects (such as plush toys or handkerchiefs) back and forth in front of her. By the time she's about three months old, these exercises will tempt her to reach out and grasp the object, a result of her budding eye-hand coordination skills.

86

give a mini-massage

If you don't have time to give your baby a
full-fledged massage, just spend a few minutes
lightly stroking him—from shoulder to wrist, thigh
to foot, and chest to tummy. You may even find that
your baby prefers this to deeper massage strokes.

87

encourage head lifts

You are the best incentive to get your baby to
practice lifting her head, which will help strengthen
her neck muscles. When she's on her tummy,
position yourself so that she'll see your face if she
lifts her head. Call her name to entice her to look
up. This exercise may frustrate some babies, so
watch for any telltale signs of distress.

3+

from three months & up

Sometimes called the honeymoon period, the second three months of your baby's life are a time of glorious smiles, belly laughs, exploring hands, and joyfully kicking feet. Many babies learn to sit during this stage, a core skill that allows them to see the world more clearly and to manipulate objects with greater precision. Most infants are picking up crucial social skills now, too, such as how to babble, giggle, and smile.

88

meet ms. spoon and mr. fork

If your baby is getting restless in a restaurant,
introduce him to Mr. Fork and Ms. Spoon. Make
the fork and spoon dance, talk, and pop out from
behind the napkin dispenser, the diaper-bag, or
the menu. Your baby will laugh and laugh—and
you'll get good practice in improvisation!

89

swing and rock

This classic poem by Robert Louis Stevenson becomes the perfect accompaniment to rocking your baby.

How do you like to go up in a swing
rock your baby back and forth gently in your arms

Up in the air so blue?
stop while holding her high on one side

Oh, I do think it the pleasantest thing
rock your baby back and forth again

Ever a child can do!
stop while holding her high on the other side

90

enchant with a music box

He won't be dexterous enough to wind a music box on his own, but your baby will enjoy hearing its tinkling tune and watching the magical twirling figurine.

91

prop up your baby

Your baby's muscle control develops from top to bottom: first her neck strengthens; then her upper back, middle back, and lower back; and finally her hips and legs. But even before her muscles can support her body, her mind focuses on the idea of sitting. (That's why she will lift her head off her diaper-changing table and pull herself up by grabbing your hands.) To help her get a start on sitting, prop her up with several large pillows. The cushioned support helps her develop balance and muscle strength, and keeps her from getting hurt if she falls over. As an added benefit, she also gets a different vantage point on the world: she's looking at life head-on, instead of from a prone position.

92

marvel at the market

At about three months of age, your baby is the perfect companion for outings to the grocery store. While he still loves to be held, he's becoming increasingly interested in the world beyond the safety of your arms. Let him ogle the colorful fruits and vegetables, smile at the butcher, and touch the frozen-food case. Introduce new words during each shopping expedition, too.

93

give her a play-by-play

While many noises interest your baby, it's the sound of the human voice that intrigues her most. Fill her ears with language by explaining what you're doing, whether it's washing her hair, making dinner, or organizing your files. She'll be exposed to new words—and to more of your world.

94

take time to listen

After the thrill of the first coos and babbles has gone, remember that your baby still needs to practice the art of conversation. To accomplish this, make sure he has opportunities to talk to a receptive audience. Give him time to untie his tongue and get some words out—even if it's just babbling.

95

put on a water show

To help your baby develop eye-hand coordination and fine motor skills, give her plastic drinking and measuring cups to play with in the tub. If she can't handle the pouring motion yet, do it for her, letting her enjoy the sight and sound of cascading water.

96

take an exercise class

Now that your baby is more settled, you can take better care of yourself. Many health clubs offer postnatal exercise classes that welcome pre-crawling infants as well. Aerobics or yoga help new mothers get back in shape. While the parents exercise, the babies enjoy listening to the music, watching the movement, and receiving the kisses, tickles, and smiles sent their way.

97

practice baby sign language

Many child-development experts believe that babies can communicate with hand signs long before they can express themselves in spoken language. In fact, some experts say that babies who learn to communicate with their hands feel more confident and are less prone to frustration than those who have no words to express their needs and feelings. Introduce your baby to nonverbal communication by teaching him a simple sign for "eat": put your fingers to your lips repeatedly each time you ask him if he's hungry, and several times during the meal.

As with spoken language, he'll probably understand the signal before he makes the sign himself, but in a few weeks, you'll see him bring his hand to his lips when he's hungry.

98

"let me touch things...
I like to feel silk, satin,
a smooth round stone,
feathers, felt, and
a rough pine cone."

99

move up and down

To demonstrate the spatial meaning of up and down, say "up" when lifting your baby and say "down" when lowering her. Use a high-pitched voice on the way up and a lower-pitched tone on the way down, so she'll start to understand that voices go up and down, too.

100

go bare

A newborn's skin may be too sensitive for this activity, but many three- to six-month-old babies love it: undress your child so he can delight in the feel of a warm breeze on his bare skin, a soft rug on his tummy, or the grass tickling his toes. As long as he's warm and not in direct sunlight, hanging out naked for a while is a great way for him to become aware of his body.

101

get bubbly

Shimmering soap bubbles, floating just beyond reach, are one of the many delights of childhood. They also serve a purpose: by watching bubbles, babies strengthen their ability to visually track and focus on objects. And by trying to touch them, they boost their eye-hand coordination.

102

whistle a tune

While talking is a long way off, your little one is tuning in to your familiar voice and starting to discern the everyday consonants and vowels that pass your lips. So surprise her by making eye contact and producing some unexpected sounds, such as briskly whistling or chirping.

103

size him up

Ask your baby, "How big are you?" Then stretch his arms gently over his head and say, "Sooo big! Sooo big!" This promotes flexibility and body awareness—and promises to make him smile.

104

roll her over

Your baby will learn to roll over at around five or six months. While this is a natural development, you can help her gain the strength, coordination, and confidence this move requires. To get her used to the motion, place her on her back on a blanket. Then gently lift one edge of the blanket so she starts to roll slowly over onto one side. After practicing this a few times, try rolling her in the opposite direction.

105

sing loudly and softly

Introduce your baby to the notion of loud and soft volumes with the popular ditty "John Jacob Jingleheimer Schmidt." Sing this verse over and over, more quietly each time, until you're just moving your lips—except for the last line, which should always be sung with loud gusto.

John Jacob Jingleheimer Schmidt,
His name is my name too.
Whenever we go out,
The people always shout,
"There goes John Jacob Jingleheimer Schmidt!"
Tah, dah, dah, dah, dah, dah, dah!

106

prepare to tap-dance

To help your baby get a sense of rhythm (as
well as a better idea of what his magical feet
can do), tap his toes along to the beat of a song.
Soon he'll start tapping and kicking his feet on
his own whenever he hears music he likes.

107

create a hand puppet

You have the makings of a puppet right at hand—actually, it is your hand. Curl your index finger into your thumb to form an O. Draw on eyes, then adopt a funny voice and move your fingers to make the face "talk." Your fascinated baby may even try to make her hand talk back!

108

introduce the big kids

If you don't have other children in your household, visit friends with older kids or spend time at the playground observing the three- and four-year-olds. Your baby will love to see what bigger, stronger kids can do. Keep him on the sidelines, rather than in the center of the action, so he's not at risk of being accidentally knocked over in all the hubbub.

109

talk to the animals

Your baby is becoming aware of both the concept of language and the differences between animals. It's now the ideal time to introduce her to the language of animals: as you both read books, play with plush toys, or greet pets, make each animal's signature noise, be it *meow, woof, moo, peep,* or *roar!*

110

make mealtime fun

Babies eat while being held in loving arms, and soon
learn that meals aren't just about food. Feedings offer
quiet times for eye contact and chats. Even before your
baby starts eating solid foods, bring him to the family
table, seated on a lap or in a highchair, and provide
unbreakable bowls, cups, and utensils to wave and
mouth, so he sees that dining is also a social event.

111

play with ice cubes

The cold temperature and slippery texture of ice cubes fascinate babies at this age. Make sure the ice is too large to pose a choking hazard. To make oversized ice blocks, freeze water in a large paper cup or milk carton, then simply peel off the wrapper.

112

sneak up on her

Why young children love a friendly game of chase is one of life's great mysteries. Many relatively immobile babies also enjoy having you creep up on them—especially if you playfully announce, "I'm gonna get you!"

113

team up on chores

Babies learn by tagging along and observing daily tasks. Don't wait until your baby is asleep to finish folding the wash. Let him sit on the floor amid the colorful clothes as you fold them, pausing to flap, shake, and discuss some items with your appreciative "laundry show" audience.

114

touch textures

Now that your baby is fascinated with tactile things, keep her tiny fingers busy with a book of textures. Look for animal-themed board books that feature fake fur. Or create a fun-to-feel book by gluing large swatches of coarse, silky, and furry fabric onto felt pages.

115

give him a lift

Your baby's perspective on the world tends to be limited to the view from the floor, crib, and stroller. But there are many interesting things higher up, too. Carry him around and show him some sights: pictures on the wall, flowers blooming on a high-twining vine, and knickknacks on your shelves. Let him stroke the fabric of jackets hanging in the closet and the cool glass of a window pane. Give him a chance to reach for snowflakes or the leaves on a tree branch. He'll get a big kick out of seeing—and experiencing—these discoveries.

116

"bolster me...
Put a rolled-up towel
under my small arms
to help strengthen
my back and neck.**"**

117

blow raspberries

Your baby will get a kick out of this silly poem. End
it by blowing a loud "raspberry" on her tummy.

Oh, it's a terrible sound
When a raspberry blows.
It's rude and it's crude
And your bad manners show!
But it sure makes me laugh
And it sure makes me giggle.
It makes my whole body
Just jiggle and wiggle!

118

click your tongue

Make loud clicking sounds with your tongue against
the roof of your mouth. This may make your baby
smile and even inspire him to try making the sounds.

119

sneeze loudly

Your infant is amazed by her body and, in particular, by the sounds she and others can make. You'll prompt a big laugh if you respond to her delicate baby sneezes with a loud, grown-up "aaaCHOOO!"

120

carry him like a flagpole

To help your baby strengthen his back and abdominal muscles, hold him facing away from you while you're standing. Put one hand just above his knees and the other hand securely under his chest. Now let him lean slightly away from your body—in a position that's similar to how a marcher carries a flagpole in a parade. Some babies enjoy being held in this angled position—so see if your child gets a chuckle from it, too.

121

introduce a new language

A child is never too young to hear a new language.
One great way to start is by greeting your baby
in the morning in both French and English with
this classic song, "Frère Jacques."

Frère Jacques, Frère Jacques,
Dormez-vous, dormez-vous?
Sonnez les matines,
Sonnez les matines.
Ding, ding, dong.
Ding, ding, dong.

Are you sleeping, are you sleeping,
Brother John, Brother John?
Morning bells are ringing,
Morning bells are ringing.
Ding, ding, dong.
Ding, ding, dong.

122

whisper sweet rhymes

During your baby's bedtime routine, dim the lights,
carry her to a window with a view of the sky,
and murmur this traditional sleeptime rhyme.

Come to the window,
My baby with me,
And look at the stars
That shine on the sea!
There are two little stars
That play hide-and-seek
With two little fish
Far down in the deep.
And two little frogs
Cry "Neap, neap, neap."
I see a dear baby
Who should be asleep.

123

sing to the tune of a classic

Introduce your child to some simple fingerplays
while singing this starry song to the tune
of "Row, Row, Row Your Boat."

One, two, three big stars
count to three with your
fingers on one hand

Blinking in the sky!
open and close both of your hands
three times to make them "blink"

Twinkle, twinkle, twinkle, twinkle
continue "blinking" both hands while
raising them over your head

How'd they get so high?
hold out your hands, palms up, as
if you don't know the answer

124

bring a sock to life

For instant baby amusement, put your hand inside a sock and open and close its "mouth" while speaking in a funny voice. This impromptu puppet show makes a great diversion when you're changing your baby's clothes or even while waiting in a long line at the store.

125

double the noise

Soft squeaky toys instantly reward your baby's
new grasping skills. Give him a toy for each
hand. Can he hold onto both yet? Does he
look at the toy that's making the louder noise?

126

explore junior-edition yoga

In baby-yoga classes, your little one lies on her
back or tummy, or in your arms, while you guide
her body into adapted poses, sometimes with
rhymes, songs, swaying, or gentle bouncing.
Several books outline the basics, though you and
your baby may enjoy the sociability of a class.

127

share family songs

Friends and family are often eager to help
new parents but may not know how. So they
might be delighted if you ask them to share
some favorite songs and rhymes that they
used to sing to their wee ones—maybe even
versions in another language. If Grandma
shares a few songs that her grandmother
sang to her as a child or that an uncle
hummed to you or your spouse, you're likely
to develop a special connection to the song
when you share it with your baby. And you
can tell him its history someday (and maybe
later he'll even sing it to his own offspring).

128

put bells on baby's toes

Buy or make socks or ankle bracelets adorned with bells and rattles. These encourage your baby to kick to hear the pleasing noise. (Make sure anything sewn onto your baby's clothing is securely fastened so it can't come off and pose a choking hazard.)

129

make a ruckus

By three months of age, your baby is able to locate the source of nearby sounds. To help her develop this skill, move around the room while talking in funny voices or making a toy squeak or rattle. Praise her efforts as she looks, squirms, and even wriggles over to the spot where you're making all those interesting noises.

130

cheer on the bouncing baby

When your baby uses your hands to pull himself upright and starts bouncing, encourage him. Many babies can do this for long stretches of time, and that's fine—it's a great way for them to strengthen their leg muscles and boost self-esteem. (There's also the benefit of giving your arms a good workout!)

131

roll for the toy

Tempt your baby to reach out and grasp things by placing a toy just off to the side of where she's lying. As she gets older, place the toy a bit farther away, which will inspire her to roll over to reach it.

132

"laugh at my giggles...
Show me that I'm a special baby
and that my joy delights you—and
how laughter, like all good things,
is best when shared."

133

start swinging

Once your baby can sit up with a bit of support, he's ready to try a ride in a bucket-seat swing. Depending on his sitting skills, you can place him toward the rear of the seat or slump him forward over the front with a rolled blanket behind him for more support. Push him gently and not too high at first—his neck may not be able to handle racing forward and backward. If he enjoys the sensation of swinging, spice up his ride by tickling his leg or kissing his cheek each time he comes forward. Swinging helps develop the vestibular system, the body's mechanism for maintaining balance and monitoring its movements. These skills are crucial for learning to crawl, walk, run, ride a bike—just about any activity that entails movement.

134

crush some chips

Stuck in line at the supermarket? Hand your baby a sealed bag of potato chips to crinkle and crush (but not to eat). She'll be diverted for at least a little while by the sound and texture of her new "toy"—a small price to pay to avoid a potential meltdown.

135

ask questions

Engage your baby by asking him questions. These can be the pleasantries of small talk: "How are you?" or "Isn't it a lovely day?" Or they can be more specific: "Are you warm in that jacket?" Wait for your baby to answer even if his response is just a string of babbled sounds. This teaches him the rhythm of conversation. In a few years, he'll be the one asking the questions!

136

vary the carrying

Car seats that can be moved from car to stroller to
house, while convenient, don't offer a baby much
physical stimulation. All infants need and love to
be held. And a baby sling is a great way for them
to travel, as a parent's arms are the safest and most
interesting place to be. After all, caring touch is
a powerful form of communication.

137

seek special recognition

Naturally you long to hear your baby say your name.
So when he babbles "ma-ma" or "da-da," respond with
a smile and say "Here's Mommy!" or "Here's Daddy!"
He'll see that some sounds net big responses.

138

appreciate books in a new way

You want your baby to look at the pictures and enjoy the cute story in her new board book, but she has other ideas: she pops the book right into her mouth. Don't worry—children's board and cloth books are made to withstand some baby gumming action. And at this stage, your child will explore much of her environment by putting things in her mouth. So let her gum books to her heart's delight. Eventually she'll explore them with her hands, eyes, and mind, too!

139

give him a concert

Your baby's fascination with sound (and with you) means that he'll be a rapt audience as you play an instrument. Experiencing how music is created—not just hearing it on a tape, a CD, or the radio—will help cultivate his interest in music. Allow him to touch the instrument. Plucking guitar strings, banging a drum, or pressing the keys of a bugle teaches him about cause and effect and lets him feel involved. And when families play music together, children learn that music is an art form anyone can enjoy.

140

sing to amuse her

Sing this endearing peekaboo song, "Where Is Baby?", to the tune of "Frère Jacques."

Where is baby?
Where is baby?
cup hands around your eyes as if searching

Where can she be?
Where can she be?
pretend to scan the horizon, searching

Where's my silly baby?
Where's my silly baby?
shrug your shoulders and put
your hands out, palms up

Ding dong dee!
Ding dong dee!
"find" your baby and give her a kiss

141

revel in quiet time

Babies are loads of fun at this stage: curious, sociable, and unbelievably cute. They love to interact, but need breaks from social stimulation, too. Don't interrupt your baby if you see her fiddling with carpet fibers, staring out the window, or playing with her toes. Sometimes she just needs time to explore the world in a quiet way.

142

give him target practice

Help your baby strengthen his leg muscles, develop eye-foot coordination, and just have fun by letting him kick at objects you hold near his feet. Use soft balls, plush toys, or whatever catches his eye and tempts his feet. For an added bonus, choose objects that make noise when struck, so your baby learns about cause and effect.

143

react to her cough

At about five months of age, lots of babies
make an exciting discovery: they learn how
to cough on purpose to get the attention of
grown-ups. Once you're sure your little actor
is coughing for effect and not because she's
ill or choking, play along with her antics. Try
imitating her after she gives a little cough,
or putting your hands on your cheeks in
wide-eyed surprise. She'll repeat her action
often to prompt your humorous responses.

144

"play a tickle game...
It's so great when you tickle and
giggle with me. My favorite part is
guessing where you'll tickle next:
fingers, toes, belly, or nose?"

145

pop a bubble

Elicit glee and giggles by blowing a big
chewing-gum bubble for your baby.
Then—*snap!*—pop it back into your mouth.

146

mimic each other

Your baby has shown you that he can stick out his
tongue and smile to copy your expressions. He may
even be imitating some of your sounds (like "ma-ma"
and "ba-ba"). Introduce a new mimicking game by
showing him how to open his mouth wide or how to
blow raspberries, then watch to see if he'll join in.

147

let her get mouthy

Allow your baby to suck on your sleeve, gum her soft blocks, and stick her big, noisy rattle in her mouth. Once you get beyond the drool factor and the fear of germs, you'll see that her mouth is one of her primary tools of exploration. So let her use it to learn about the world—just make sure that nothing sharp, toxic, or small enough to swallow is within reach.

148

turn up the volume

As your baby begins to babble, he'll also start experimenting with the volume of his voice. Without startling him, show him how your own voice can get louder—as well as quieter. He may follow right along.

149

talk about body parts

By frequently repeating the names of body parts to your baby, you'll help her learn what her body does and build her receptive vocabulary (the number of words she understands). Try to use body-part names in the course of everyday speech, rather than in a dull recitation. For example, instead of saying "These are your toes, and these are your hands," try something like "Let's get these little toes into your socks," or "Are your hands sticky?"—and emphasize the word you are teaching her. This builds her vocabulary and introduces more complex sentence structures.

150

kiss the toes

Your baby will giggle with delight if you
recite this ditty while kissing his toes.
One, two, three, four, five
Hey, baby! These toes are alive!

151

play with parachutes

Babies and young children love experimenting with
fabrics—whether it's a scarf billowing high above
a child's head or a huge lightweight cloth that kids
pull over themselves to create a canopy. To make a
parachute suitable for your baby, drape a sheet, scarf,
or thin blanket over your tiny adventurer's head, then
whisk it off again—sometimes quickly, sometimes
slowly. She'll enjoy this tactile version of peekaboo.

152

make a mobile that's mobile

Even though your baby's ability to focus on things in the distance is improving, he'll often prefer to look at details nearby. To provide a choice, securely attach colorful, lightweight objects to the stroller cover so they dangle just out of his reach. Keep them on top of the cover while he enjoys the scenery, and flip them down into view when he gets restless.

153

create light shows

Help your baby strengthen her focus and visual tracking abilities by shining a flashlight on the wall in a darkened room. Try moving the light up to the ceiling, then down the wall, creeping closer to her. She may even try to reach out and touch the light!

154

rhyme in the rain

Singing in the rain to your bundle of joy is great fun with favorites like "Little Ducky Duddle."

Little Ducky Duddle
went wading in a puddle,
wading in a puddle so small.
Said he, "It doesn't matter
how much I splash and splatter,
I'm only a ducky, after all."

155

boogie to the music

Dance with your baby to lively music. Have someone stop the music and yell, "Freeze!" Stop dancing—and watch his face light up at the sudden change. When the music starts again, resume dancing. Repeat this stop-and-start routine—he'll giggle each time you stop.

156

encourage crawling

Your infant may be wriggling across the floor
or rocking back and forth on her hands and
knees with a clear desire to get moving. Help
her get the front of her body and the back end
working together by placing desirable objects,
such as favorite toys, just out of her reach. This
encourages her to be aware of objects as well as
of her own body, and tests out her pre-crawling
skills. Soon her urge to grab the objects will
overcome her confusion about the mechanics
of how to get there—and she'll succeed!

157

bounce for balance

It may seem impossible for a baby to develop a sense of balance when he has just two main positions: lying down and sitting. The key is making sure he has plenty of opportunities to move around, too. Spinning, rocking, and bouncing all develop the vestibular system in the inner ear, which is responsible for a sense of balance and an awareness of where the body is in space. To gently stimulate that part of your baby's ears, put him on a bed (lying down, sitting, or "standing" with support) and very gently bounce the mattress.

158

play footsie

Combine gentle tickles with this playful rhyme.

Shoe a little horse
pat the bottom of your baby's right foot

Shoe a little mare
pat the bottom of your baby's left foot

But let the little coltie go bare, bare, bare!
tickle the bottoms of both feet

159

tickle her fancy

Try another little rhyme with a ticklish finish.

Round and round the garden, with my teddy bear
circle your baby's belly with your index finger

One step, two step—tickle her under there!
"walk" your fingers up and tickle under her chin

160

prepare him to crawl

Put your baby on his tummy for this pre-crawling exercise. Gently push one foot toward his body, then the other. He'll learn to push his foot against your hand, which will thrust him forward—ever so slightly at first. As he gets used to the exercise, he'll cover more ground with each push and get a clearer idea of how this crawling business actually works.

161

explore a garden

While babies can't tell the difference between tulips and ferns, they recognize a beautiful place when they see it. Spend time with your baby in gardens or parks; she'll be enchanted by the waving branches, colorful blooms, singing birds, and wonderful smells.

162

"what a big world this is...
Tell me about everything I
see—from your funny red hat
to that large black cat.**"**

163

toss a beach ball

Enchant your baby with the motion and color of
a gently tossed inflatable beach ball. Lay him on
his back, then throw the ball in the air and catch it
above him—again and again. He'll love watching
it sail through the air—and he'll enjoy the surprise
of seeing you catch it just before it reaches him.

164

saddle up for a knee ride

Sit your baby facing toward you on your knees, and hold her securely around her middle as you treat her to a lively—but gentle—knee ride. As she rides, vary your tempo, pitch, and volume.

The farmer's horse goes ho-dee-ho, ho-dee-ho
gently sway your baby forward and backward,
as if she's on a very fat, waddling horse

The lady's horse goes trip-trop, trip-trop
alternate bouncing each knee
slowly up and down

The gentleman's horse goes trot-trot, trot-trot
simultaneously bounce both knees
quickly up and down

But (say your baby's name) *horse goes
gallopy, gallopy, gallopy, gallopy!*
alternate bouncing each knee
quickly up and down

165

pop like popcorn

Your baby will smile at this sprightly fingerplay,
even though he's too young to eat popcorn.

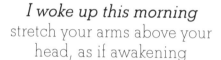

I woke up this morning
stretch your arms above your
head, as if awakening

And what did I see?
frame your eyes with your hands
as if looking through binoculars

Popcorn popping on my apple tree!
quickly raise and lower your arms several
times while opening and shutting
your hands (like popping corn)

Spring has brought me a big surprise
continue to raise and lower your arms while
opening and shutting your hands

Popcorn popping right before my eyes!
continue opening and shutting your hands

166

trot like a pony

Hold your baby securely on one knee. Gently raise it up and down as you chant this English nursery rhyme.

Ride a cockhorse to Banbury Cross
To see a fine lady upon her white horse.
With rings on her fingers and bells on her toes,
She shall hear music wherever she goes.

167

rock out

Infants enjoy listening to much more than so-called baby music. Experiment with a variety of lively songs from your own music collection to find out what your child likes most. Encourage your little dancer to kick and wave her arms whenever you turn on the tunes.

168

entertain with sounds

Your babbling baby enjoys repeating sounds. But he might be surprised to hear you do the same. Try repeating, with gusto, a single, fairly silly word (like "banana"), for a startled reaction or maybe a belly laugh from your little linguist.

169

teach her to sit

It takes some time for babies to learn how to balance on their bottoms well enough to sit. You can help your infant gain stability by putting her legs in a diamond-shaped position. Move her heels closer to her bottom, bending her knees out to the sides. With a wider base, she's less likely to topple.

170

fashion a toy-blanket

At the local toy store, you've probably seen play-blankets with sewn-on flaps, unbreakable mirrors, and assorted fabrics. These toy-blankets enliven tummy-time and encourage reaching and scooting. You can make your own by sewing together large squares of colorful, assorted, very tactile fabrics—velvet, corduroy, fleece, vinyl, satin, or canvas. (Make sure the pieces are all washable, and prewash them before assembling.) Sew the patchwork onto a heavyweight piece of cloth as a backing. Stitch on a few loops to firmly secure rattles, the back covers of cloth books, and teething rings. Then let your baby explore this easily portable play area.

171

swing around the clock

Your baby will enjoy swinging from side to side like the pendulum of a cuckoo clock, even if he won't be able to tell time for years to come.

Tick tock, tick tock
hold your baby securely under his arms and gently swing him from side to side

I'm a little cuckoo clock.
continue swinging

Tick tock, tick tock
continue swinging

Now I'm striking one o'clock.
lift your baby above your head one time

Cuckoo! Cuckoo!
swing him from side to side

repeat by adding two o'clock and three o'clock, and lifting up your baby two and three times, respectively

172

have fun with fingerplays

Add hand gestures to the song "Yankee Doodle"
to make it even more fun for your little one.

Yankee Doodle went to town,
"walk" the fingers of one of your hands
across the palm of the other

A-riding on a pony,
pretend to hold onto the reins of a bridle

Stuck a feather in his cap
mime sticking a feather in a hat

And called it "macaroni."
whirl your index finger around in a circle

6+

from six months & up

By now your baby is a charmingly social creature, one who laughs and calls out to provoke a response or win your attention. He's also a mobile baby who can roll over, and is beginning to creep, crawl, and pull himself up to get what he wants. He will test his emerging fine motor skills by fiddling with his toys or food. And he's starting to understand that objects exist even when they aren't visible: a conceptual milestone that lets him be an active participant—rather than a spectator—in hiding games like peekaboo.

173

take a rainy-day walk

Grandma may scold; a neighbor may shake his
head. But letting your baby feel a little rain on a mild
day is perfectly safe, perfectly legal, and perfectly
delightful. It stimulates her sense of touch, smell,
and taste, and can promote bonding as you and
your baby explore the wet world beyond your front
door. Make sure her rain gear keeps her warm and
dry—only her face and hands should be peeping out!

174

create a rainbow

Show your baby how a prism can turn sunlight into a shimmering rainbow. Hang the prism in front of a bright window, or hold it in your hand and make the light dance around the room. Or try adjusting a glass of water on a sunny windowsill until it creates a rainbow (which he might try to grab) on the floor.

175

make a family photo album

Strengthen the bond your baby feels with the rest of her family by filling an album with photos of people she knows and loves. Add pictures of beloved pets and toys, too, and you'll have a book that will engage and entertain her for years to come.

176

go barefoot

Once your baby starts standing up with your assistance, you may be tempted to keep shoes on his feet whenever he's not napping. Going barefoot, however, is the best way for an infant to learn how his little feet work. It also makes it easier for him to figure out how to rock back and forth to find the "sweet spot" that gives him balance, because he'll be able to feel the subtle contractions of the muscles that keep him upright.

Slip nonskid socks on your baby's feet if they are cold, and put shoes on if he's treading anyplace where sharp objects might be present. But if he's indoors or outdoors on a safe surface, he'll be fine going barefoot.

6+

6 months & up

177

march with the duke

"The Noble Duke of York" is sure to elicit giggles as your baby accompanies the Duke on his adventure.

Oh, the Noble Duke of York. He had 10,000 men.
sit on the floor with your legs extended in front of you and gently bounce your baby on your knees

He marched them up to the top of the hill,
slowly bend your knees upward, with your baby seated on them

And he marched them down again.
slowly lower and straighten your knees

And when you're up, you're up,
raise both knees

And when you're down, you're down,
straighten both legs

And when you're only halfway up,
raise both legs halfway up and pause

You're neither up nor down!
move legs up and down quickly

178

introduce activity books

Now that your baby's fine motor skills are more developed, he'll love opening the flaps, pushing the buttons, and stroking the fake fur featured in children's activity books. Actively engaging with books—not just passively listening to the words—helps an infant develop a love of reading that can last a lifetime.

179

play tug-of-war

Give your infant one end of a cloth diaper or blanket to hold, then pull gently on the other end. As she pulls, increase your resistance a tiny bit. This gentle tugging game helps her develop upper-body strength and a sense of success. (Just don't pull so hard that she'll tumble backward if she lets go!)

180

track the toy

While your baby can now track objects passing back and forth before his eyes, it's not until about his seventh month that he'll be able to follow items moving up and down. (If you drop something in front of a younger baby, he won't look down for it.) Move a toy slowly up and down about 10 inches (25 cm) in front of him. See if he can follow it; if he can't, try again in a few weeks.

181

experiment with sound

If your little percussionist enjoys banging on pots, treat her to a new sound by swirling a cup or two of water in a metal mixing bowl while one of you strikes it with a metal spoon. The moving water extends the bang into a wavering tone worthy of science fiction.

182

fly a kite

Few toys are as magical to a child as a
colorful kite soaring in the sky. While
carefully supervising, allow your baby
to touch the tugging string and see
how it leads up to the dancing kite.

183

jump to it

This game gives your baby a perfect blend of reassuring repetitions with a dash of surprise. Hold him braced against your chest, slowly chant "1...2...3...jump!" and finish with a sudden hop. Repeat, but vary the tempo, speeding up the counting, or slowing it down to create suspense leading up to the final hop.

184

ring the doorbell

As your baby turns into a reckless explorer, keep quick, easy amusements on tap, such as the doorbell-distraction game. Simply scoop her up, go to the front door, and demonstrate the magic of the doorbell. Show your baby how she can press the button herself—she'll be wowed at how she can fill the place with sound.

185

blow water bubbles

Using a straw, blow bubbles in a glass of water. The turbulent motion will catch your baby's attention, and the gurgling sounds will intrigue him. Don't let him try this trick himself, though, as he could poke himself with the straw or inhale the water.

186

give her a security blanket

Many infants adopt what developmental psychologists call a "transitional object." It's usually a blanket or plush toy, and it gives the child something that—unlike people—doesn't come and go. So let your baby cling to, suck on, sleep with, and drag around her special object as much as she likes, since it provides a sense of continuity and reassurance.

187

explore the looking glass

Hold your baby in your arms as you stand in front of a mirror and ask, "Who's that?" Although he won't yet understand whose reflections he's seeing, he'll love looking at the smiling, happy faces.

188

listen up!

In this auditory version of hide-and-seek, stand behind your baby while she's playing on the floor. Call out "Where's Mommy?" or "Where's Daddy?" then wait for her to turn around and locate you. When she goes back to playing, call out again from a different location behind her.

189

6+

6 months & up

"encourage me to sing...
I may just gurgle,
I may just shout,
but it's really music
I'm learning all about."

190

take baby steps

Hold your baby securely under his arms with his face looking away from you, then set his feet on top of yours and walk slowly with small steps. He'll be thrilled to experience the joy of walking.

191

perform scarf tricks

You don't have to be a magician to pull off this trick—and you'll be helping your baby work on her fine motor skills and eye-hand coordination. Simply stuff a lightweight scarf into a paper-towel tube. Then—*voilà!*—show your baby how to pull it out. Now put it back in and let her tug it out herself.

192

blow a kiss

It may take a year or two before your beloved baby can master the art of blowing a kiss. But when you blow a kiss to him, he'll understand that you're sending affection his way—and he may even enjoy trying to emulate your actions.

193

listen to rain sticks

When turned upside down, these South American musical instruments—long tubes filled with beads, dried beans, or pebbles—sound like a rain shower; when shaken, they make an intriguing rattle. Rain sticks provide both auditory stimulation and the opportunity for your little rainmaker to practice her fine motor skills.

194

squeeze the sponges

Give your bathing beauty a variety of body scrubbers such as loofahs, bath mitts, and natural sponges to play with in the tub or a big basin of water. Squeezing water out of the sponges will stimulate his sense of touch and strengthen his small hands. (Always remember to closely supervise water play.)

195

introduce tactile treats

Whip up a batch of colored gelatin and place either cubes or spoonfuls on your child's highchair tray. Then watch as your aspiring artist creates abstract sculpture by smearing, rolling, squishing, squashing, and smashing the shimmering stuff.

196

meet mr. knickerbocker

It will be a few more months before your baby can make all the sounds in this chant, but she'll love the rhythm and enjoy watching you go through the movements.

Hey, Mr. Knickerbocker, boppity bop!
pat your hands on the floor once, clap, repeat

I like the way you boppity bop!
continue patting and clapping to establish a beat

Listen to the sound we make with our hands.
rub your palms together

Listen to the sound we make with our feet.
stomp your feet on the floor to the beat

Listen to the sound we make with our knees.
tap your fingers on your knees to the beat

Listen to the sound we make with our teeth.
click your teeth together

197

devise a distraction

Rather than fight your baby's urge to grab things at
the grocery store, give him a bag of marshmallows,
a box of macaroni, or a carton of tofu to examine,
squeeze, and shake while he sits in the shopping cart.
The novelty of these impromptu "toys" will keep him
happily occupied (while still under your watchful eye).

198

listen for clues

Hide an object that makes noise—a ticking clock,
a music box, or a talking plush toy—where your
adventurous crawler can find it. As she searches
for the source of the sound, she'll be testing her
auditory tracking skills. She'll also gain a sense of
mastery when she discovers the little noisemaker.

199

follow the falling leaves

Watching the twirling motion of falling leaves and hearing them crunch as the two of you step or roll on them will fascinate your baby. Let him try to catch the leaves as they fall—even if he never actually captures them, he will hone his eye-hand coordination.

200

babble with your baby

Have you noticed how your baby tends to say her "words" in a series, such as "ba-ba-ba" and "ma-ma-ma"? Expand her listening skills and sound repertoire by introducing her to new sounds, like "ta-ta-ta" and "la-la-la." Then wait for her to respond. You're starting to teach her the art of conversation!

201

knock 'em down

Your baby is not old enough to construct block towers yet (that typically happens around 16 months of age), but he will enjoy using his hands to knock over structures that you build for him. The sight—and sound—of crashing blocks will entice your little demolition expert to do it repeatedly, so be prepared for a busy construction schedule!

202

crawl together

Many babies think it's hilarious to follow a crawling parent around the house or yard—so indulge your newly mobile explorer. (And by getting a baby's-eye view of the world, you may see safety hazards you hadn't noticed before.)

203

play dropsie

As your infant gains more control of her hands and a better understanding of what they do, she'll discover the age-old game of dropsie. The rules are simple: baby drops object on the floor; parent picks it up. Baby drops object again; parent picks it up again. Tedious, right? But look at it from your baby's point of view: she's showing you that she understands she has power over objects and can influence people's behavior—and that's a huge cognitive leap forward for babykind.

6+

6 months & up

204

" raise me up...
I love it when you help me pull myself up so I can stand—again and again and again!**"**

205

build a blanket fort

Remember the makeshift forts you loved so much when you were a kid of six or seven? Babies also appreciate a cozy hideaway—especially if a parent or sibling hangs out with them. Simply drape a couple of large blankets or sheets over a table or two tall chairbacks, and crawl underneath with your little camper.

206

dine in the buff

Even the most adorable baby clothes lose their appeal when they're covered in oatmeal or puréed peas. So let your baby eat in the buff once in a while. Not only will it keep his clothes stain-free, but it's also fun for him. And when he smears carrots across his chest, remember that he's becoming more aware of his body.

207

go jogging

Whether you're running or walking, you'll get great exercise pushing your baby in a jogging stroller, and she'll love feeling the wind in her hair. Wait until she's about six months old, when her neck muscles are strong enough to withstand the jostling. Use a stroller made for jogging; it will have better shock absorption.

208

shake it up

To graduate beyond infant rattles, make "big-kid" noisemakers by filling plastic storage containers with assorted objects: jar lids, spoons, wooden blocks (nothing small enough to be a choking hazard). Snap on the lids and listen as he shakes, rattles, and rolls.

209

sing about ducks

With its counting, quacking, and mother-child story line, "Five Little Ducks" is always an engaging tune.

Five little ducks went out one day
hold up your hand and wiggle five fingers

Over the hill and far away.
Mother duck said,
"Quack, quack, quack."
hold your hands palm to palm, then open
and shut them three times while saying "quack"

But only four little ducks came back.
hold up your hand and wiggle four fingers; repeat
stanzas decreasing the number each time until
you get to "none of the little ducks came back"

Sad mother duck went out one day
wiggle one finger

Over the hill and far away.
The sad mother duck said,
"Quack, quack, quack."
hold your hands palm to palm, then open
and shut them three times while saying "quack"

And all five little ducks came running back!

210

explore a fabric tunnel

A collapsible cloth tunnel (available at specialty toy stores) will tempt novice and experienced crawlers alike. Crawling through it will teach your baby about spatial relations, and if you add a toy inside, she'll discover that there's even a prize at the end of the tunnel!

211

add funny words

By about six months of age, babies have developed quite a sense of humor. Many can even appreciate simple word games: try adding a gorilla to the lyrics of "Old McDonald," or singing "kitty" instead of "baby" in the song "Rock-a-Bye Baby"—and watch the smiles begin.

212

hide in plain sight

If your baby easily finds toys hidden under boxes or blankets, challenge his sense of perception by concealing a toy behind a transparent barrier, like a clear cutting board or a plastic picture frame. Does he try to get the toy by reaching through the cutting board or frame—or by reaching around it?

213
horse around with hats

Your baby's fascination with her own image, plus her dawning awareness that she's a unique individual, will make her a rapt audience if you set her in front of a mirror and have her model some hats. Fancy ones are fun, but even a baseball cap or a straw gardening hat will do nicely.

214
turn to the flip side

Tape a bright, simple picture to a big, plain box and show it to your baby. Once you've engaged his attention, encourage him to find the picture by turning the box around. He might scoot or crawl around the box, chasing the picture that he watched you make disappear.

215

tease and tickle

This game introduces your baby to the
names of body parts—and works well
as a diaper-changing distraction.

Bug-a-boo's got feet, feet, feet
lightly tickle your baby's feet

Bug-a-boo's got shins
flutter your fingers up his legs

Bug-a-boo's got a mouth to eat
pat your fingers on his mouth

And Bug-a-boo's got chins!
give him a quick tickle under his chin

216

give the teddy kisses

Your baby will model your behavior, even when the action is directed at, say, a teddy bear: "Here's a kiss for Teddy!" and "Here's a kiss for Baby!"

217

teach him to feed himself

Do you spend more time trying to stop your baby from grabbing his spoon than actually feeding him with it? Then it's time to start letting him take over. Load a child-size spoon with a sticky food that won't slide off, such as oatmeal; put the spoon in his hand, and guide it to his mouth. He'll be feeding himself with a utensil on his own in the second year.

218

spray for fun

Babies love new sensations, and being sprinkled on the tummy with cooling drops of water is a particularly refreshing one. Use a clean squirt bottle to spray your baby with a fine mist of water.

219

count it up

This classic counting rhyme will prime your baby for when she learns numbers later on.

One, two, buckle my shoe.
Three, four, shut the door.
Five, six, pick up sticks.
Seven, eight, lay them straight.
Nine, ten, do it again!

220

greet him on the fly

Next time you're pushing your baby on a playground bucket swing, enhance the physical fun by cheerfully saying "bye" when you push the swing up and reuniting with a happy "hi" when the swing comes back to you. He may not understand the words, but he'll notice the repeating sounds, and may kick his feet in anticipation of the next push of the swing.

221

bathe with buoyancy

Collect assorted floating objects—like waterproof toys and empty plastic bottles (tape caps securely shut)—and set the little flotilla adrift in the bathtub. Your little sailor will love watching them bobble and hearing you name and describe any objects she manages to catch.

222

"follow my lead…
My preferences are important,
so when I'm ready to play ball,
I hope you'll be ready to play
ball with me, too!**"**

223

permit peaceful moments

In the hustle and bustle of life with a baby, it can be difficult to balance work, play, and exercise with quiet time. Try to indulge in peaceful moments with your child—whether you're sitting on the lawn listening to birds sing or just lying on the bed watching the ceiling fan spin around. Quiet time gives you and your baby a chance to relax and bond in a deeper way than when you're rushing between places and activities.

224

look up, up, and away

Point out birds, butterflies, planes, and other winged wonders to your baby to elevate his perspective.

225

make a book

Even at this tender age, babies begin to express their interests. One may be enamored of ducks, another of trees, and another of bananas. Indulge your baby's fancies by making a book about her favorite subject. Punch holes in several pieces of cardboard, string them together with yarn, and paste in pictures from magazines or even your own drawings. As she grows older, this type of book conveys the idea that a single thing can be portrayed in many different ways.

226

spoon it out

Raid the utensil drawer for large spoons and spatulas that your baby can wave, bang, and lick. Show him how to pass a spoon from hand to hand, which will teach him how to grasp with one hand while releasing with the other—no small feat for a baby.

227

row your boat

Take your baby for a make-believe boat ride to the tune of "Row, Row, Row your Boat." Sit with your knees bent and your feet flat on the floor. Position your little sailor with her back against your tummy. Gently rock forward and back as you hold her hands and "row" together. The rocking will stimulate her vestibular system (which helps her balance)—and work your abs!

228

sing a highchair song

Belt out this ditty (to the tune of "Shortnin' Bread") whenever you're about to feed your baby—especially if he's a little cranky.

Sittin' in my highchair, highchair, my chair
Sittin' in my highchair, banging my spoon
Bring on the jelly, bring on the bread
Somebody get this baby fed.

Sittin' in my highchair, highchair, my chair
Sittin' in my highchair, banging my spoon
Bring on the carrots, bring on the peas
Somebody feed this baby, please!

6+

6 months & up

229

meet the animals

You may not be ready to bring
home a pet goldfish, guinea pig,
puppy, or iguana, but your baby
will love seeing the animal world
in action. A well-stocked pet store
can provide almost as much fun
as a zoo, because babies are as
captivated by a domestic mouse
as they are by an African lion.

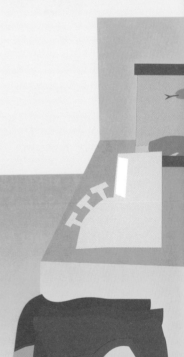

230

get wet

If the weather's warm enough, pour a shallow amount of water into a large tub or kiddie pool outside and let your baby splash around. Add small plastic watering cans, buckets, and rubber ducks for more fun—but never leave her alone, not even for a minute.

231

pull a switcheroo

Stand in front of your baby and hold a small puppet or plush toy behind your back. Bring it out in front of you and show it to your baby, using first your left hand, then your right, then your left again. Soon you'll be able to tell by his expectant gaze that he's anticipating which hand will have the toy. Try varying the pattern you use. Can he anticipate that one, too?

232

make merry music

Music takes on new meaning when your baby learns about making it with other people (not just listening to it). Pick up a recorder or drum; hand her a tambourine or rattle. Even if you're only able to *ting-ting* a triangle, you'll both love the music that you make together.

233

stock up his drawer

At age six months and up, babies develop a pattern: see, grab, and let go. Rather than chastising your curious one for doing what comes naturally, fill a low drawer with items he can explore whenever he wants. Stock toys, cups, unused sponges, or whatever is on hand that's safe and easy for him to handle.

234

expand your storytime talk

Hearing books read aloud is important for all kids—even those who are already reading on their own. But reading the printed words isn't enough. Expand your baby's vocabulary and introduce new ideas by talking about what's on the page, such as the various colors and shapes. This type of storytime discussion will engage your child for years to come.

235

kiss with gusto

Babies learn that kissing is a sign of affection, and they start kissing back at about eight months of age. Encourage your little smoocher by asking "Who wants a kiss? Who wants a kiss?" Then make an exaggerated sound as you plant one on her cheek.

236

"let me hang out with babies...
Although I can't play with
them yet, I'm fascinated by
other people my size."

237

knock his socks off

It's inevitable: once your baby figures out how to pull off his stretchy little socks and expose his toes, he'll do it repeatedly. This activity gives him a precious sense of self-determination and helps build coordination. So go ahead and applaud his efforts. As long as it's not cold, it's okay to bare those tootsies.

238

say "thank you"

Her emerging awareness of social relations means that she'll get a kick out of the simple game of handing you toys and hearing you say "thank you" again and again. Besides entertaining her, this little ritual introduces her to a core concept of etiquette: expressing gratitude.

239

fill up the jar

Once your baby can sit up on his own, give him a plastic jar with an extra-wide mouth and some small, age-appropriate toys. Guide his hand and show him how to put the toys into the jar; this teaches him about spatial relations ("How much stuff fits in here?"). Then demonstrate how to remove the toys, which boosts his problem-solving skills ("How can I get these toys out?").

240

give a juggling lesson

With a toy in each of her hands, what will your baby do if you offer her a third toy? Will she try to grab it with her hands full? Or drop everything? In time, she'll put down one toy before grasping another.

241

try a new peekaboo

You and your baby have likely gotten hours and hours of pleasure from playing the classic game of peekaboo, in which you cover and uncover your face with your hands. Try a new version the next time you change your child's diaper: instead of hiding your face, place a clean diaper on your baby's face. When he reaches out to pull it off, help him remove it, and exclaim, "Peekaboo!" This game helps him understand that both you and he still exist even when he's "hiding."

242

teach the sign for "drink"

Babies can learn signs long before they learn to speak, and this early signing is believed to help them acquire spoken language more easily. So teach your baby some signs, such as this one for "drink": curl your hand as if you are holding a cup and bring it to your lips. Make this motion every time you give your baby a drink. Soon she'll do it herself to show you that she's thirsty.

243

phone home

If your baby watches you intently during your phone conversations, let him in on the mystery. The next time you talk to a caller he knows well, put the phone up to his ear so he can hear that familiar voice. Soon he'll be ready to babble some replies.

244

buzz with the bees

Babies love the bee sounds in this rhyme,
especially when they're accompanied
with a little tickling action.

Here is a beehive.
make one of your hands into a fist

Where are the bees?
make an "I don't know" open-palm
gesture with the other hand

6+

6 months & up

Hidden away where nobody sees.
hide your fist behind your back

Soon they will come,
Creeping out from the hive,
bring your fist in front of you again

One, two, three, four, five!
open your fist one finger at a time

Buzzzzzzzzzzz! Buzzzz!
tickle your baby

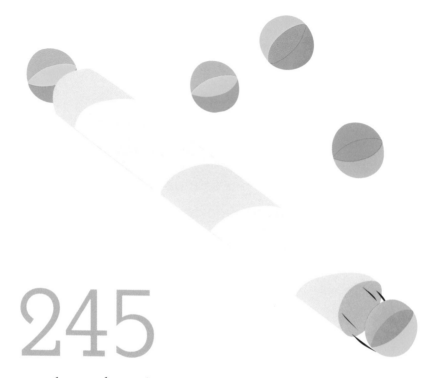

245

make the balls disappear

Put on a magic show for your baby by rolling some balls
through a cardboard tube. She'll be fascinated as she
watches the balls disappear—then suddenly reappear.
This trick will also teach her about object permanence
(the idea that an object doesn't cease to exist just
because it's not visible) and spatial relations (the way
some things, like balls, fit into other things).

246

present some pasta

Put a spoonful of cool, wet, cooked spaghetti on your baby's highchair tray. He'll enjoy trying to peel apart and squish the slippery strands.

247

feel the fruit

You've just come in, and you need 10 minutes to put away the groceries. So plunk your little one down on the kitchen floor and present some play-worthy produce to engross her, within your field of vision, while you finish your task. She'll love how the rough-skinned cantaloupe and the sweet-smelling oranges roll in funny, unpredictable ways.

6+

6 months & up

248

bend those knees

Even after your baby has mastered the fine art of pulling himself up to a standing position by holding onto the nearest object—be it an armchair or your leg—he may be unsure how to get back down on the floor. You may find his bewildered look adorable at first, but after he's called you over and over, it loses some of its charm. To teach him how to lower himself without falling, gently push behind his knees to make them bend. Then guide him down and slightly forward until he ends up on his knees. After a few days' practice, he'll be pulling himself up and plopping down with ease.

249

record her voice

As your child starts to understand that she is actually a separate person (a concept that fully develops when she's 12 to 15 months old), hearing her own voice will thrill her. Record her gurgling, babbling, and giggling, then play it back for her. This also will give you an audio scrapbook of some of your baby's first sounds.

250

share a laugh

This is the age when babies start laughing at their own humor. The "joke" may be dropping a toy on the floor over and over, shrieking at passersby, or making open-mouthed faces. Whatever tickles your baby's fancy, let it tickle yours as well. Laughing at his jokes shows him that he has the power to amuse people.

251

find the sheep

This classic nursery rhyme is particularly appealing to babies if you use a plush sheep to act out the story.

Little Bo-Peep has lost her sheep
And doesn't know where to find them.
Leave them alone
And they'll come home
Wagging their tails behind them.

252

bang away

Set a metal, rimmed cookie sheet on the floor in front of your baby or on his highchair tray, then give him a selection of hard objects, such as wooden blocks, metal spoons, and plastic cups. Help him drop the objects onto the sheet. Which bang does he like best?

253

"let me play with the lights...
On, off, on, off, on, off—
look what I can do!"

254

give her a hand

By six months, many infants are ready to learn to clap. Gently hold your baby's hands between yours and clap them together while chanting a nursery rhyme such as "Patty Cake." Eventually she'll get the hang of the routine and start clapping on her own.

255

sock it away

Play with your baby's budding understanding of object permanence (that an object exists even when it isn't visible) by placing a small toy in an adult-size sock. Show him how you pull the toy out by reaching your hand inside the sock. Before you know it, he'll begin to look in the sock for the missing toy himself.

256

sing a song of teeth

Clean those emerging first teeth and surrounding gums with a wet thin washcloth, a piece of gauze, or a baby toothbrush—no need for toothpaste just yet. Introduce this cleaning routine in baby steps: open your own mouth wide to encourage imitation; then start with just one quick, shallow swipe in your baby's mouth. You can get more thorough as the action becomes familiar. Add some fun to the routine by singing this song to the tune of "Here We Go 'Round the Mulberry Bush":

This is the way we brush our teeth
Brush our teeth
Brush our teeth
This is the way we brush our teeth
So early in the morning!

6+

6 months & up

257

search for the baby

When you pull a shirt over your child's head,
at the moment her face is hidden by the shirt, ask
enthusiastically, "Where's the baby ?" When her face
reappears, say "There she is!" Vary the game by lifting
her over your head while you pretend to search for her,
then bringing her face-to-face for a cheerful reunion.

258

hop for fun

He can't jump, he can't walk, and he may not even be
sitting on his own yet, but your baby will be thrilled to
hop up and down in a jumpy seat—and his legs will get
stronger with each takeoff and landing. Clamp the seat
onto an extra-wide door frame so he has plenty of room
to move around, and stay nearby to ensure his safety.

259

pop open an umbrella

Babies make an easy-to-impress audience. From
your baby's viewpoint, for example, an umbrella
mysteriously transforms—with a click and a swoosh—
from a long, wrinkled object to a smooth, colorful
expanse. So open an umbrella in front of her with a
bit of drama and say: "Open sesame!" followed by
a quick Mary Poppins–style twirl of the umbrella.
You'll win her entertainer-of-the-year award!

260

create a crawl course

Once your child masters the art of crawling,
set up an easy obstacle course where he can
hone his problem-solving abilities and practice
the gross motor skills that his newly acquired
mobility requires. Choose an area with a soft
rug, or roll out a mat or blanket to cushion
his hands and knees. Set up small cushions
and piles of blankets for him to clamber over;
be ready to give him a boost over obstacles if
he needs it. Drape sheets over chairs to create
tunnels to crawl through, and hide toys for
him to discover along the way.

261
drum it up

Hold off on the drum set until your baby is a teenager—or at least until she can sit up by herself! In the meantime, let her pound away on other percussive objects, like saucepans and plastic containers. Early exploration of sound teaches her about rhythm.

262
lavish him with kisses

By now, your baby is old enough to see the joy in kisses that depart from the norm. Try an Eskimo kiss (rubbing noses), a butterfly kiss (fluttering your eyelashes against his cheek), and an angel kiss (lightly kissing his eyelids). Before long, he'll be kissing you back in a variety of ways.

263

make a splash

The game of dropsie takes on a whole new meaning when you add water. Partially fill a bathtub, then give your baby waterproof toys and balls to drop into it. The resulting splash will delight her, and the actions she's performing will develop her eye-hand coordination, exercise her grasp-and-release skills, and demonstrate cause and effect. (Always closely supervise water play.)

264

feast on finger foods

Once your baby can feed himself, encourage him to practice this skill by laying out bite-sized morsels that you can enjoy together. This allows him to show off his all-important pincer grasp using his forefinger and thumb—and bask in a special meal just with you.

265

describe the world

The more you talk, the more your baby will hear, and the more words she'll store in her memory. Providing a running commentary on everyday life introduces her to the rhythms of speech. Through this, she'll begin to understand the world around her and how people explain things to each other. Someday you'll hear her telling her teddy something in the same tone you used to explain it to her—and you'll know she was listening.

266

go bottoms-up

Lie on your back, with knees bent and feet flat on the floor, and lay your baby on your shins, facing you. Holding him snugly, curl your knees toward your nose until he's horizontal or tip him slightly bottoms-up.

9+ from nine months & up

At this age, even those babies who aren't yet walking are beginning to look and act like toddlers. Games that allow your child to practice gross motor skills—crawling, pulling himself up to stand, cruising across the floor, or climbing—are particularly appealing to him now because mobility is his main objective. Fine motor skills are also important to him. He may insist on turning the pages of a book or stacking blocks on his own. Get ready: this is the beginning of the do-it-myself stage.

267

play peekaboo with toys

Reinforce the concept of object permanence (the idea
that objects exist even when they aren't visible) by
making a big show of hiding a toy under a blanket
and then helping your child find it. Soon she'll learn
to recognize shapes by the hidden toy's outline—for
instance, the telltale lump of her plush bunny. If she's
having trouble finding the toy, cover just part of it.

268

pull out a laundry basket

Chances are you already own one of the world's most versatile baby toys: the laundry basket. It makes a perfect fort, playpen, or doll crib. Your baby can also throw toys in it and push it around, or climb in and have you pull him across the floor. Someday you may even get to put laundry in the basket again!

269

hop to it

You can stimulate your child's sense of balance using a large vinyl "hopping" ball with a handle (sold at toy shops and sporting-goods stores). Although her feet can't yet touch the ground when she's on the ball, have her hold the handle. Bounce the ball gently with one hand, keeping her upright with the other.

270

play hide-and-seek

After months of experimenting with the concept of object permanence (the notion that objects exist even when they aren't visible), your baby is finally ready for the big time: a game of hide-and-seek, where both baby and grown-up get to do the hiding and the seeking. But don't do a really good job of hiding, because that might frustrate or scare your baby. Instead, help him by calling out, "Come find me! Where am I?" This game isn't just fun for babies—it also helps them work through separation anxiety as they see you "return" after your "disappearances."

271

master the stairs

Although it's tempting to turn stairs into a forbidden zone, it's better to teach your baby how to navigate them safely. Climbing up doesn't take much practice, but to go down safely, she needs to turn onto her belly and lower her feet down onto each step below her. Once she learns how to feel for a solid object behind her feet, she'll have the foundation not only for stair-climbing but also for later pursuits, such as scrambling around a play structure as a preschooler or scaling rocks as a teenager. Always make sure the stairs' safety gates are securely closed when your baby is not practicing her climbing under your supervision.

272

introduce push toys

Even before he masters alternating his legs
to propel himself on a riding toy, your child can
push himself with both legs at once. This pushing
action allows him to strengthen his muscles and
experience the joy of independent mobility. Stay
nearby, as your baby may still need a helping
hand to keep him balanced and safe.

273

bring out the brushes

Water play in all forms will be a hit for years to
come with your little one. On a warm afternoon,
give her some dollar-store paintbrushes and a
bucket of water, and let her "paint" the sidewalk.

274

get out the muffin pan

Once your baby has mastered the ability to pick up
and release objects, he'll enjoy plopping tennis balls,
toys, and wads of crumpled-up paper into the cups of
muffin tins—an action that hones fine motor skills.

275

stuff a box

Cut a large hole in the lid or side of a shoe box, then
show your baby how to stuff toys through the hole and
into the box. She'll learn about the relative sizes
of toys and about object permanence (the fact that an
object still exists even when it's not visible). Picking
up and pushing toys through the hole will also help
her develop her fine motor skills, as will sticking her
hand into the hole to take the toys out again.

276

smell intriguing scents

Gather some small plastic containers, such as film canisters, and look in your pantry for some strongly scented ingredients to insert inside each container. For example, saturate a cotton ball with vanilla extract or crumple a cinnamon stick. Put one ingredient into each container, close and tape it securely shut, then poke holes in the lid. Let your baby sniff the scents.

277

steer a baby wheelbarrow

This activity strengthens your child's upper body and develops his coordination: pick up him by his hips or under his chest so he can "walk" on his hands. When he's older and stronger, hold up his feet instead.

278

visit the zoo

If your baby crows over animals seen in the distance and in books and has enjoyed visits to pet stores, seek opportunities for her to see new species and perhaps even touch some live critters. Visit a petting zoo to introduce her to the amazing creatures that inhabit our planet. Be sure to supervise your little one's interspecies meeting, and wash her hands afterward.

279

give him a lift

Let your child experience the joy of motion with this up-in-the-air game. Sit on a carpeted floor with your baby facing you. Lift him up and, while holding him firmly, roll back so that he "flies" over your head. This action strengthens his back and stimulates the vestibular system, which helps him balance. It's also likely to prompt a lot of giggles from your copilot.

280

soar down the slide

At first, your baby may want to go down the kiddie slide only with your help—guiding her from the side and catching her at the end. Over time, however, as she feels safer, she'll want to whiz down all by herself.

281
sort the shapes

With a shape-sorter toy, first show your child how the round piece fits into the round hole, then show him how the square and triangular pieces fit into their matching holes. Soon he'll be matching up the shapes himself. This activity teaches spatial relations and shape discrimination, and develops fine motor skills.

282
encourage early walkers

The primary challenge of walking is finding one's balance. To help your toddler-to-be get up—and stay up—give her objects that provide resistance and stability but are light enough for her to push. A laundry basket filled with clothes works well. Avoid baby walkers and tricycles, however, as they roll too quickly.

283

"watch home movies with me...
I like to see all the fascinating
people—especially Mommy
and Daddy and that cute
baby—doing fun things."

284

teach the concept of size

Your baby will enjoy trying to imitate you as
you do the hand gestures of this simple rhyme.

Big fish, little dish
hold your hands out wide, then cup them together

Big log, little dog
hold your hands out wide, then close them together

Big rug, little bug
stretch your arms out, then put your index
fingers and thumbs close together

Big sky, little guy
open your arms up wide, then hug your baby

285

construct a cardboard condo

An older baby's love of child-sized spaces, the peekaboo game, and imitative play means that he'll be thrilled to have his own house—be it ever so humble. Get a big box from an appliance store, cut out windows and a door, and decorate the exterior with paint and stickers. Tuck blankets and toys inside to create a cozy retreat for the new tenant.

286

draw together

It will be a few years before your baby can draw anything even remotely resembling, well, anything. Still, she'll enjoy drawing lines with a crayon, marker, or piece of chalk. If she can't do it herself, hold her hand gently in yours and guide it on the paper.

287

bedazzle with balloons

When your baby tugs on the strings of helium-filled balloons, he'll be greatly intrigued at how his movements make the balloons bounce all around. Choose Mylar balloons; unlike latex ones, they don't pop, so they're less likely to be ingested. Always supervise balloon play and make sure that the strings are short so your baby doesn't get tangled in them.

288

give encouragement

Praise—in the form of "You're such a good girl!"
or "What a smart girl!"—generally focuses on the
child herself. Encouragement, on the other hand,
is aimed at a child's efforts: "You really worked hard
to get up that hill!" or "I'm amazed at how fast you
can run!" Most experts agree that encouraging a
child is preferable to praising her, because praise
sets the child up for wanting to always be "smart,"
"good," or "strong," whereas, encouragement
focuses on the child's actions and not her worth
as a person. Start boosting your baby's sense
of competence now, as she's becoming aware of
herself as a separate being who needs to be
recognized as both lovable and capable.

289

get tools for tots

Older babies and toddlers are keenly interested in imitating the grown-ups in their lives, so you may find your little one trying to brush his own hair, sweep up crumbs, or bang a hammer. Keep him safe yet satisfied by giving him toy versions of the tools you use around the house. Whether he's fiddling in a play kitchen or puttering in a pretend workshop, this initial imitating behavior will evolve into full-fledged fantasy play later on, in which armchairs serve as pirate ships and leaves are ingredients for a magic potion.

290

stack the rings

Your child won't be able to stack colored rings on a plastic toy pole in order from large to small until she's closer to age two. At this stage, urge her to use her budding problem-solving skills and eye-hand coordination to stack the rings in any order—and to enjoy what she does best now: take things apart!

291

cut to the chase

Whether he's waddling around on two feet or zipping around on all fours, your baby will love an active game of chase. Keep it gentle—you don't want to frighten him—but motivate him with words of encouragement, funny noises, and lots of laughter. Then change it around so he gets to chase you, too.

292

burst the bubbles

Your baby has always loved to watch you blow soap bubbles, and at about nine months of age, she's now ready to reach out and pop them. So encourage her! She'll practice her eye-hand coordination—and she will feel proud of her popping performance.

293

dial his number

Fascinated by the ringing and all the buttons, your baby may already be grabbing for your phone. End the power struggle by giving him one of his own. Whether it's a toy or an unwanted cordless phone, pretending to use it will make him feel like Mommy or Daddy. At the same time, he'll get to practice his language and social skills.

294

talk into a tube

If your child is intrigued by sounds—especially the
funny ones she makes herself—then talking (or
rather, babbling) through a tube might be a lot of fun
for her. Pick up a paper-towel or wrapping-paper tube
and show her how to talk, blow, hum, and sing
through it. Then let her take a turn.

295

give him a backpack

When he sees an older sibling—or a caretaker—using
a backpack, your little one will probably want to
have one, too. Although he can't wear a pack until
he's a steady walker, he'll enjoy helping you fill
his personal pack with toys, snacks, or books—and
then dumping them out again.

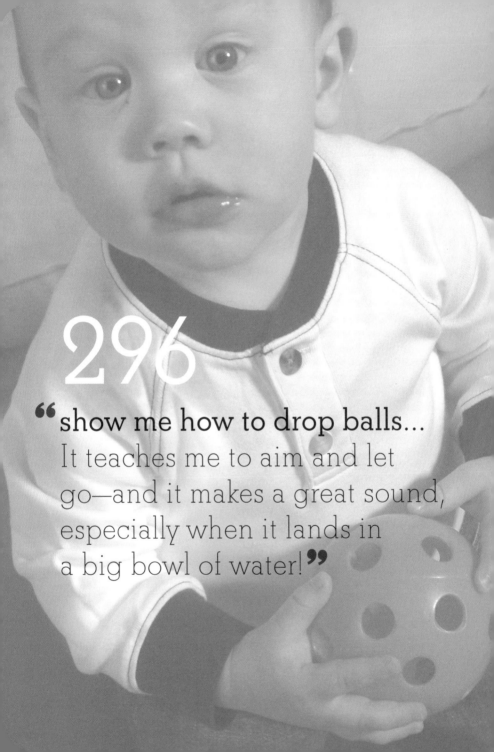

296

"show me how to drop balls...
It teaches me to aim and let
go—and it makes a great sound,
especially when it lands in
a big bowl of water!"

297

take turns

Your child will jump at the chance to practice walking by pulling or pushing a sturdy wagon. Take turns with her: first give her a ride in the wagon, then have her give her small charges (dolls and plush toys) a ride.

298

challenge his balancing skills

Kids love to test their balancing skills by trying to crawl or walk along wide beams in parks and at children's play centers. They can enjoy such balancing acts at home, too: simply lean a broad, firm board up against a low, sturdy chair or table. Make sure the floor underneath is cushioned. Then, as you stand beside him or hold his hand, encourage him to crawl or walk up and down the board.

299

play jack-in-the-box

This old-fashioned toy, with its tinkling tune and pop-up puppet, continues to delight kids, even the very young. Help your baby turn the handle and stuff the puppet back into the box after it pops up—but no one needs to teach her how to laugh when that puppet magically greets her again and again!

300

wrap him up

Unroll about 4 feet (120 cm) of wrapping paper on the floor and plop your baby in the middle of it. He'll enjoy rolling on it, tearing it, crackling it, and pulling it across his body. Just make sure he doesn't tear off any pieces and put them in his mouth, as they could pose a choking hazard.

301

bathe the toy babies

Set up a small tub with warm water and soap suds
to give your baby a chance to bathe her own "babies,"
whether they're dolls, rubber duckies, or plastic
dinosaurs. Remember to supervise her at all
times, and keep a towel on hand for spills.

302

take a dip

And he thought his little bathtub was fun! From
the safety of your arms, your little swimmer can
learn to feel comfortable in the wide-open space
of a pool. Bounce through the water together while
he revels in the sensation of weightlessness and
discovers the joy of kicking and splashing. (Never
leave your child unattended in or near a pool.)

303

get cheeky

In the realm of simple baby pleasures, squashing a parent's puffed-out cheeks between two hands ranks high, especially if you act very surprised each time your baby does it.

304

pour another one

Your baby sees you pouring liquids all day long: a cup of coffee for yourself, some milk into her bottle, or water into the cat's bowl. From her perspective, this looks like a lot of fun. So give her a turn: when she's in the tub, let her practice pouring with sippy cups and plastic bottles. She'll develop an awareness of size and volume while sharpening her fine motor skills.

305

explore the world on foot

If your baby's walking, provide him with plenty of
opportunities to amble down the sidewalk, meander
along a dirt path, or waddle across a grassy lawn.
He sharpens his powers of observation as he picks
up rocks and sticks, listens to his shoes tapping on
the concrete, and stops to examine scurrying bugs.

306

give puppet kisses

Don a small hand puppet and use it to give "kisses" to different parts of your baby's body. She'll love to hear you tell her where the puppet is going to kiss her next.

307

sing for your supper

Make mealtime even more fun for your wee one by reciting this time-honored rhyme as he enjoys his food.

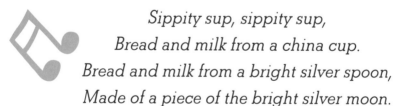

Sippity sup, sippity sup,
Bread and milk from a china cup.
Bread and milk from a bright silver spoon,
Made of a piece of the bright silver moon.
Sippity sup, sippity sup,
Sippity, sippity, sup!

308

wave bye-bye

Saying good-bye is one of the first social rituals babies learn because it's a gesture they can easily recognize and copy. By teaching your child about language ("bye-bye!") and routines (the action of waving every time someone leaves), you establish a soothing ritual that might help her if separation anxiety is making departures difficult.

309

play ball

Balls are an all-time favorite toy. Give your child a variety of different-sized balls and notice how he adapts his play for each one. Demonstrate the possibilities: throwing, rolling, bouncing, catching.

310

sing "where is thumbkin?"

Borrowing the melody of "Frère Jacques" and adding some peekaboo fun, this fingerplay will amuse your baby well into her preschool years. Start with both of your fists behind your back.

Where is Thumbkin? Where is Thumbkin?
Here I am.
bring your right hand out with your thumb up

Here I am.
bring your left hand out with your thumb up

How are you today, sir?
bend your right thumb as if talking

Very well, I thank you.
bend your left thumb as if talking

Run away.
put your right hand behind your back

Run away.
put your left hand behind your back

continue with "Pointer," "Middle Finger," "Ring Finger," and "Pinkie"

311

let 'er rip!

Before you toss out your monthly magazines,
hand one or two to your baby to explore something
different: the thrill of tearing out the pages! The
ripping action sounds great and helps him develop
both gross and fine motor skills. Watch him closely
to make sure he doesn't put any paper in his mouth.

312

broaden your circle

Schedule get-togethers with other parents and babies.
Even though your baby won't play with other children
until she's near the end of her second year, she'll
enjoy watching and imitating them. And you'll learn
from observing other babies—and parents, too!

313

reverse the roles

At about nine months, babies start imitating the
grown-ups and older kids in their lives and enjoy
giving them some personal attention. So encourage
your child to put food in your mouth, dab your face
with a washcloth, and brush your hair. It makes
him feel like a big person and allows him to be
the nurturer, not just the one being nurtured.

314

give her a foot rub

Feet are wonderfully sensitive to touch. Treat your
active baby to a relaxing foot massage before she goes
to bed. Softly rub the bottom of each toe, then make
circular movements on her heels with your thumbs.
For a more soothing massage, use a child-safe lotion.

315

"show me creepy crawlies...
I like to watch worms wiggle
around, big bugs crawl up and
down, and ants run all around."

9+

9 months & up

316

play at the beach

With plenty of sun protection and supervision, the beach makes a wonderful destination for you and your baby. He can dig in the sand, slap the water, watch the birds, and go for a dip—in an adult's arms, of course.

317

point out the body parts

Share this classic children's song with your baby by demonstrating the movements as you sing. Then repeat the song and help her focus on her own body parts by guiding her hands to the appropriate places.

Head, shoulders, knees, and toes
touch your hands to these body parts in order

Knees and toes!
pat your knees and toes

Head, shoulders, knees, and toes
touch your hands to these body parts in order

Knees and toes!
pat your knees and toes

Eyes and ears and mouth and nose
touch your hands to these body parts in order

Head, shoulders, knees, and toes
touch your hands to these body parts in order

Knees and toes!
pat your knees and toes

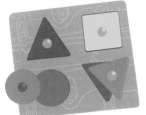

318

puzzle it out

Exercise your baby's spatial-relation and fine motor skills with durable wooden puzzles. Start with a basic circle-shaped puzzle with only one piece; once he masters that, graduate to a puzzle with a few more pieces. Look for easy-to-grasp knobs, bright colors, and matching pictures or patterns on the board that will help him determine where each piece goes. Show him how to slide the pieces into place.

319

hide the toy

Tie a long ribbon onto a favorite small toy, then let your baby watch as you hide the tethered plaything under the sofa. Help her pull the ribbon to bring the toy back into view. Can she retrieve the toy by herself?

320

elaborate on his past

Talking about what has happened in the past helps build your baby's capacity to remember. But don't just talk about common occurrences or ask questions with "yes" or "no" responses, such as "Did you have a yummy snack today?" Instead, elaborate on activities and relationships. For example, each day, talk about what you did together, where you went, and the people you saw: "When we played with your friend Carter at the park, a big black dog licked your toes!" In time, as you repeat the more memorable stories, your child will begin to build what psychologists call an "autobiographical memory."

321

stack the containers

Show your baby how to balance different-sized plastic containers on top of each other, and how to nest the small containers inside the big ones. This activity teaches spatial relations and how to discriminate between various shapes and sizes. Remember, she'll knock things down before she learns to stack them.

322

give blanket rides

A blanket ride is much like a sled ride, except that you pull a blanket across a floor or grass instead of a sled across snow. Sit or lay your child on a blanket, then gently pull the blanket. Try different directions. If you add an older child to the mix, he can ensure that the baby doesn't topple over, plus this doubles the fun!

323

shuffle the magic cups

A slower, simpler version of the classic shell game can be challenging and fun for babies. Show your child that you're putting a small toy or ball under a plastic cup. Then turn over a second cup. Slowly move the cups around. Now ask her to find the toy. She may not get it right away, but if you move the cups very slowly, eventually your baby will be able to guess correctly. (You might try playing with only one cup first to help her understand the game.) This activity will strengthen her visual tracking abilities and expand her powers of concentration.

324

read it one more time

Familiarity breeds contentment in babies, even if
the same old same old gets a little, well, old for
grown-ups. Try to stay cheerful even if you've read
that board book about trains 101 times in the last two
weeks. The repetition helps your baby associate words
with pictures, an essential step in developing both
language and reading skills. And knowing what's
coming on the next page makes him feel secure.

325

show her yellow

As your child learns to sort objects by characteristics,
color becomes increasingly important. Try having a
yellow day: point out all the yellow objects you see.
Green, orange, and purple days are sure to follow.

326

stack the rocks

Everyday objects often make the best toys, and a favorite among many babies is a simple pile of dirt-free rocks. They're fun to stack, push over, and hit together. Choose lightweight, medium-sized rocks that won't pose a choking hazard.

327

teach him rhythm

Research shows that babies can perceive rhythms and anticipate what comes next in a pattern, even if they can't always replicate that pattern. Try this yourself by demonstrating a simple rhythm, like clap-clap-rest, clap-clap-rest. Watch as your baby tries to imitate this rhythm. Pattern recognition is key for learning to talk, read, do math, and appreciate music.

9+

9 months & up

328

"roll the ball to me...
I can stop it with my hands,
and that helps me get more
coordinated—and ready for
playing with a friend someday."

329

quack like a duck

Animal sounds, hand gestures, and one bossy
duckling make this song a sure winner.

Six little ducks that I once knew,
hold up six fingers

Fat ones, skinny ones, fair ones, too.
make hand motions for "fat" and "skinny"

But the one little duck
hold up one finger

With the feather on his back,
wiggle your fingers near your back

He led the others
"walk" fingers of one hand across the palm of the other

With a "quack, quack, quack,"
open and close your hand like a duck bill

a "quack, quack, quack."
open and close your hand like a duck bill

He led the others with a "quack, quack, quack."
open and close your hand like a duck bill

330

take the route less traveled

An obstacle course can help your toddler develop balance and eye-foot coordination. Arrange small blocks or a broom handle to crawl or step over, hula hoops to go in and out of, a jump rope laid out in a wavy pattern to follow, and cushions to clamber over. Give her a hand if she needs one: the point is to help her develop as a walker, not to test her.

331

ride a rocking horse

Your little cowboy will love rocking himself back and forth on a plastic pony or classic wooden steed. Set the horse on plush carpet or grass and always stand by, just in case the bronco bucks.

332

rearrange the furniture

The cruising phase—when babies hang on
to furniture or human legs for support as they
shuffle from one spot to another—is crucial in
learning to walk, as it gives babies a chance to
practice taking steps. Help your child cruise by
creating a chain of sturdy furniture that runs from
one side of the room to the other. Move fragile
objects, such as lamps, wobbly end tables, or
plant stands, away from her eager grasp. This
may make your room look a little odd, but
most babies go through the cruising stage
relatively quickly. And her glee at being able
to get around on her own two feet will make
the decorating disruption worth it.

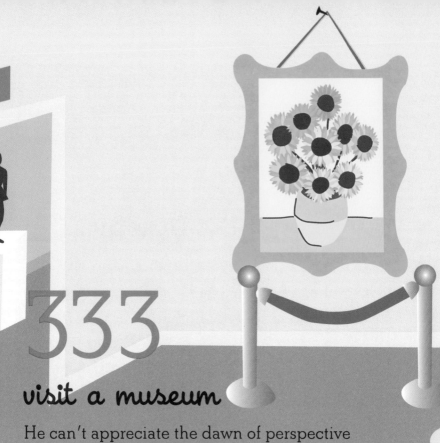

333

visit a museum

He can't appreciate the dawn of perspective during the Renaissance, or the odd things that happened to human figures during the Cubist period, but your inquisitive child will still marvel at the colors and forms on display in an art museum. And the halls between galleries are a great place for him to practice his early walking skills. Try to avoid peak hours—and break up the art tour with visits to a café and the outdoors so he doesn't get bored or overstimulated.

334

revel in quiet reading

Reading to your little one is crucial for developing her love of books. And if she is showing even the slightest interest in looking at books alone, let her enjoy them on her own. It shows that she can entertain herself and that her attention span is increasing.

335

enjoy the magic of magnets

Need to occupy your curious one while you're cooking or cleaning? Place a variety of large colorful magnets on the bottom portion of your refrigerator door or on a magnetic board. He can experiment with sliding them around, peeling them off, putting them back on, and sticking them together. (Avoid small magnets that can pose a choking hazard.)

336

sing the color song

Help your baby learn about basic colors by singing this song as you point out examples of each color, like the red sock, the green ball, and the very blue fish.

Red and orange, green and blue
Shiny yellow and pink, too.
I love colors, and I love you!

337

record a book on tape

When you leave your child with a babysitter, ease his separation anxiety by recording yourself reading one of his favorite books. He'll love hearing your voice when you're not there, and listening to the familiar words will comfort him. For nap time, record several books in a row for him to listen to as he falls asleep.

338

wrap old favorites

Your baby might enjoy seeing some old friends. If you loosely wrap a few of her old favorite toys in wrapping paper, her play can start with crinkling the paper and ripping it open . (Just don't let it become a snack!)

339

climb the ladder

Crawling and climbing are similar cross-lateral movements—one is horizontal and the other vertical. Show your baby how to move his hands and feet up the rungs of a ladder, such as the one on a slide. Stand behind and below him, and guide him the whole way. Soon he'll be clambering up the ladder all by himself.

340

enjoy a knee ride

Seat your baby on your knees facing you, then hold
her securely for this gentle but bouncy ride.

Down by the banks of the Hanky Panky
gently bounce your baby up and down on your knees

Where the bullfrogs jump from bank to banky
lift your baby onto one knee, then onto the other knee

With a hip, hop, hippity hop
gently bounce your baby up and down on your knees

Jump off the lily pad, and kerplop!
while holding your baby securely, gently
lean her backward as if she's falling

341

invite the toys to tea

Once your baby learns the purpose of using a cup, demonstrate how to give his teddy bear or doll an occasional "sip" of his water or (pretend) tea. He may laugh or even copy this bit of make-believe—a small precursor of all the imaginative play ahead.

342

water the plants together

Your baby loves to imitate you, and she's fascinated with water. So what better way to amuse her than by letting her water some outdoor plants? Hold her hands on a watering can or—for even more fun—use a hose. Of course, most of the water will go on her feet (and yours) and not on the plants, but she'll enjoy feeling like a big person—and getting a bit wet!

343

walk tall

Congratulate your aspiring little walker with this charming song about one of life's most amazing milestones. Sing it to the tune of "I'm a Little Teapot."

I'm a little walker, I walk tall.
Sometimes I stumble, sometimes I fall.
But now I'm two-legged, so hear me call:
"I'm walking tall and having a ball!"

344

bring out old-timers

Even though your baby has outgrown his infant toys, the rattles can delight him in new, exciting ways. Make a game by hiding them in a shoe box, assembling a rattle "band," or stacking them up.

345

"dance with me...
I may rock, sway, or just nod my head, but however I dance, I'll learn about rhythm and self-expression.**"**

346

give her an earful

Long loved as a camp and hiking chant, "Do Your Ears Hang Low?", with its accompanying hand motions, can also entertain infants who are learning about ears.

Do your ears hang low?
tug on your earlobes

Do they wobble to and fro?
quickly wiggle your earlobes

Can you tie them in a knot?
mime tying a knot

Can you tie them in a bow?
mime tying a bow

Can you throw them o'er your shoulder
mime throwing something over your shoulder

Like a Continental soldier?
salute and march in place

Do your ears hang low?
tug on your earlobes

347

teach "simon says"

Your baby's too young to play this game by the rules
of the playground set. But a simplified version will teach
him to listen to verbal directions and organize his body
in order to follow them. Use simple commands at first,
such as "Simon says touch your toes" or "Simon says
open your mouth." Always demonstrate what you want
your baby to do so he can try to imitate you.

348

grab for gadgets

Your baby is at the peak age for seeking out everyday
objects, such as cups, plastic hangers, and boxes.
These simple household items are just as effective as
top-of-the-line developmental toys for practicing her
fine motor skills and indulging in imitative play.

349

build a sand castle

He'll need help making the basic structure, but your young architect can pack a pail full of sand all by himself or just pile on handfuls of the stuff. The tactile stimulation of sand is irresistible, and the teamwork sets the foundation for future cooperative play.

350

run interference

Can't keep your baby from reaching into the waste basket or unrolling the toilet paper? You say "no" over and over, but temptation still gets the best of her. Try saying "no" to the undesired behavior just once or twice, then distract her with something equally intriguing. If she's digging in the trash, for instance, hand her a basket of toys to search through.

351

say "good night"

To ease bedtime transitions, walk around the house with your baby saying good night to familiar objects: "Good night, teddy bear. Good night, couch. Good night, toothbrush. Good night, Mommy's bed," and so on. This creates a soothing ritual for your baby and helps expand his vocabulary.

352

touch and talk

Help your baby develop tactile awareness. Fill a large, wide-mouthed plastic jar with items that have a very distinctive feel, like a plush dog, a plastic fish, and a rubber ball. As your baby enjoys pulling each object out of the jar, talk about what she's touching: "This dog is so soft!" and "Does that fish feel funny?"

353

meet the animals

Older babies, who are intrigued by the sounds and adventures of animals, get a kick out of "The Animal Fair"—especially if you sing the song on the way to the zoo or circus.

I went to the Animal Fair.
The birds and the beasts were there.
The big baboon by the light of the moon
Was combing his auburn hair.

You should have seen the monk.
He sat on the elephant's trunk.
The elephant sneezed and fell on his knees
And that was the end of the monk,
The monk, the monk, the monk.

354

play with pretend food

Given your baby's emerging interest in imaginative play and his budding ability to feed himself, try having a pretend meal with him, using plastic food and utensils. Choose large pieces of "food" that don't pose a choking hazard.

355

pedal away

When your baby reaches her first year, she's ready for the thrill of joining you on a bicycle ride—as long as she's wearing a helmet and sitting snugly in an approved child's seat or trailer. Travel on bike paths or well-paved roads with minimal traffic, and stop often to talk about the sights—and to check on her.

356

flip some lids

Let your baby practice his manual-dexterity skills on a couple of large plastic storage jars with screw-top lids. Start by just resting a lid on top of a jar. Show him how to screw the lid on and off, and then let him try it.

357

do broom pull-ups

To strengthen your baby's hands, arms, upper torso, and back, hold a broomstick horizontally in front of her, have her grasp the stick with both hands, then slowly lift her a few inches off the ground (so she doesn't fall far if she lets go). At first she may not be able to hold on, but after some practice your little gymnast may be able to suspend herself at least partially. Do this exercise over a soft surface, such as a large floor pillow.

358

play a silly name game

Though they can't yet talk and have likely never seen a stand-up comic (except for you!), babies nine months and older can understand silly-sounding words or phrases or even a good joke—especially if the joke's about them.

Is your name Muffin Head?
put your hands on your head

Is your name Mr. Ed?
turn your palms upward and shrug your shoulders

Is your name Doodlee Doodlee Doo?
tickle your baby's tummy

Is your name Bug-a-Boo?
"walk" your fingers up your baby's chest like a bug

Is your name (say your baby's name)?
turn your palms upward and shrug your shoulders

It is?
wave your hands in the air excitedly

Hurray!
clap your hands

359

remember the first words

Whether he says "aye" for hi, "oggo" for go, or "ope" for toast, make a list—or even a recording on tape or CD—of your baby's first words. It will bring back sweet memories for you and your family in later years—and delight him when he's older, too!

360

massage her head

When your little one is in a quiet mood, pamper her with a head massage. Gently stroke her face along the bridge of her nose, then across her brows to her temples. Next, stroke from her nose across her cheeks. Finish by massaging along the sides of her face, including her ears, and finally the back of her head. Repeat this if she's enjoying your tender touch.

361

pair up the shoes

Turn that jumble of shoes in your entryway or closet into a learning experience. Hand one shoe to your baby and ask him to help you find its mate. Start with one pair; as your baby masters the game, add more.

362

introduce the talking heads

Puppet shows can be an effective tool for demonstrating how conversations work, whether they are between a puppet and your baby or among the puppets themselves—or both. These shows can also model appropriate expressions of emotions. As your child gets older, she may want to speak through the puppets and have them say things she'd be afraid to say herself. Encourage the dialogue.

363

go, speed racer

Lean a board or piece of cardboard against a chair or stair. Demonstrate for your baby how fast his wheeled toys can go down the ramp. Then it's his turn.

364

create a messy masterpiece

Provide your petite Picasso with the ingredients to make an artwork: place a pile of whipped cream on her highchair tray, then add a drop or two of food coloring. Show her how fun it is to swirl and smear the whipped cream with her hands all over the tray! Pull out the camera to document her performance art.

365

plan a picnic

Warm sun, happy butterflies, chirping birds,
a soft blanket, and delicious snacks—frankly,
even the ants will enchant your baby at a picnic.
The cuisine may not be sophisticated, but it's the
company (you!) and the fresh air that counts.

9+

9 months & up

index

a, b, c

"All the Pretty Little Horses," 74
"The Animal Fair," 353
Animals, 29, 109, 229, 278, 353
Art, 195, 286, 333, 364
Backpacks, 295
Balance, 49, 157, 169, 176, 269, 298
Balloons, 287
Balls, 82, 142, 163, 222, 245, 269, 296, 309, 328
Baths, 51, 52, 194, 221, 263, 301
Beach fun, 316
Bedtime, 56, 122, 351
Bells, 79, 128
Bicycle rides, 355
"Big Fish, Little Dish," 284
"A Birdie With a Yellow Bill," 8
Blankets, 23, 170, 186, 205, 322
Blinking, 39
Blocks, 201
Blowing, 30, 33
Body awareness, 20, 53, 100, 103
Body parts, naming, 14, 44, 144, 149, 215, 317, 346
Bolstering, 116
Books, 36, 138, 178, 225, 234, 324, 334, 337
Bouncing, 63, 130, 157, 258, 269
Boxes, 275, 285, 348
Bracelets, 79, 128
Broom pull-ups, 357
Bubbles, 101, 145, 185, 292
"Bug-a-boo's Got Feet," 215
Car rides, 46, 47
Carrying, 18, 120, 136
Chasing games, 112, 291
Cheek game, 303
Children, watching other, 108, 236, 312
Chores, 69, 113, 247
Clapping, 254, 327
Climbing, 271, 339
Clothing, 10, 81, 173

Colors, 48, 325, 336
"Come to the Window," 122
Coughing, 143
Counting, 209, 219
Crawling, 20, 156, 160, 202, 210, 260
Cruising stage, 332
Crying, 62
Cups, 323, 341, 348

d, e, f

Dancing, 22, 106, 155, 345
Daydreaming, 35
Diaper changes, 25, 30
Distractions, 88, 134, 197, 233, 247, 350
Doorbell, 184
"Down by the Banks," 340
"Do Your Ears Hang Low?" 346
Dropping games, 203, 252, 263, 296
Encouragement, 288
Exercise, 96, 207
Eye contact, 11, 39, 85
Faces, 3, 27, 41, 75, 78
"The Farmer's Horse," 164
Feet, 53, 54, 150, 158, 176, 237, 314
Fingerplays, 58, 123, 165, 172, 196, 310
"Five Little Ducks," 209
Flashlights, 59, 153
Floor gym, 83
Flying games, 24, 279
Forts, 205, 268
"Frère Jacques," 121, 140, 310

g, h, i

Good-bye, 220, 308
Hammocks, 49
Hands, 42, 71, 79, 97, 107
Hats, 213
"Head, Shoulders, Knees, and Toes," 317
Head lifts, 87, 91
Heartbeats, 1
"Here Is a Beehive," 244

"Hey, Mr. Knickerbocker," 196
Hiding games, 212, 214, 231, 241, 245, 255, 267, 270, 319, 323
Hopping, 183, 258, 269
"How Do You Like to Go Up in a Swing?" 89
Humor, 211, 250, 358
"Hush, Little Baby," 21
Ice cubes, 111
"I'm a Little Walker," 343
Imitating, 19, 41, 76, 78, 146, 168, 211, 289, 312, 313, 327, 342, 347, 348
Insects, 315
"Is Your Name Muffin Head?" 358
"Itsy-Bitsy Spider," 58
"I Woke Up This Morning," 165

j, k, l

Jack-in-the-box, 299
Jars, 239, 276, 352, 356
"John Jacob Jingleheimer Schmidt," 105
Journals, 73
Kicking, 128, 142
Kisses, 26, 64, 150, 192, 216, 235, 262, 306
Kites, 182
Knee rides, 63, 164, 166, 177, 266, 340
Laughing, 132, 250
Laundry baskets, 268, 282
Lights, 153, 253
"Little Bo-Peep," 251
"Little Ducky Duddle," 154
Lullabies, 21, 22, 38, 74
"Lullaby and Good Night," 38

m, n, o

Magazines, 311
Magnets, 335
Massages, 40, 53, 86, 314, 360
Mealtime, 88, 110, 206, 217, 228, 246, 264, 307, 354

Memory, 320
Mirrors, 3, 187, 213
Mobiles, 48, 57, 152
Mouth, putting things in, 138, 147
Movies, 283
Muffin pans, 274
Museums, 333
Music
   box, 90
   dancing to, 22, 106, 155, 345
   listening to, 12, 167
   making, 139, 189, 232
"The Noble Duke of York," 177
"Now We're Washing," 51
Object permanence, 245, 255,
   267, 270, 275
Obstacle courses, 260, 330
"Oh, Baby's on My Knee," 63
"Oh, It's a Terrible Sound," 117
"One, Two, Buckle My Shoe," 219
Outdoor activities, 5, 6, 161, 173,
   199, 230, 305, 316, 365
Outings, 70, 92, 229, 278, 333
Overstimulation, preventing, 4, 84

p, q, r

Parachutes, 151
Patience, 77
Patting, 17
Peekaboo, 55, 140, 151, 241, 257,
   267, 310
Perspective, changing, 72, 115, 224
Phones, 243, 293
Photo albums, 175
Physical contact, 17, 18, 22, 28, 34,
   80, 136
Picnics, 365
Pinwheels, 33
Plants, 161, 342
Pouring, 304
Praise, 288
Puppets, 107, 124, 299, 306, 362
Puzzles, 318
Quiet time, 35, 141, 223, 334

Rain, 154, 173
Rainbows, 174
Rain sticks, 193
Rattles, 50, 68, 79, 128, 344
Reaching, 68, 101, 131, 240
Reading, 36, 234, 324, 334
Rhythm, 61, 106, 327, 345
Ribbons, 43, 319
"Ride a Cockhorse," 166
Riding toys, 272
Rings, stacking, 290
Rocking, 61, 89, 331
Rolling over, 104, 131
"Row, Row, Row Your Boat," 95, 227
"Round and Round the Garden," 159

s, t, u

Sand castles, 349
Scarves, 191
Shapes, 281
"Shoe a Little Horse," 158
Shoes, 176, 361
Sign language, 97, 242
"Simon Says," 347
"Sippity Sup," 307
Sitting, 91, 169
"Sittin' in My Highchair," 228
Sit-ups, 66
"Six Little Ducks," 329
Size, 284
Slides, 280, 339
Smell, sense of, 45, 276
Smiling, 32, 76
Sneezing, 119
Songs, sharing, 127
Sounds
   hearing, 31, 50
   locating, 9, 129, 188, 198
   making, 13, 102, 109, 117, 118, 119,
      125, 128, 146, 148, 168, 181, 184,
      193, 196, 208, 252, 261, 294
Spoons, 226
Stacking, 290, 321, 326
Stairs, 271

Standing, 176, 204, 248
Stretching, 16, 23, 103
Strollers, 152, 207
Surroundings, changes, 60, 65
Swinging, 49, 89, 133, 171, 220
Talking
   to baby, 2, 13, 37, 93, 99, 135, 148,
      149, 162, 200, 265, 320
   first words, 137, 359
   practicing, 94
   recording, 249
Tea party, 341
Teeth, 256
Telephones, 243, 293
Textures, 7, 98, 111, 114, 170
Thank you, 238
"This Is the Way," 256
"This Little Piggy," 54
Tickling, 14, 15, 144, 158, 159, 215, 244
"Tick Tock, Tick Tock," 171
Transitional objects, 186
Tug-of-war, 179
Tunnels, 210
Umbrellas, 259

v, w, y, z

Vision, stimulating, 9, 31, 48, 67
Visual tracking, 27, 29, 85, 101,
   153, 180, 323
Wagons, 297
Walking, 190, 207, 282, 297, 305,
   330, 332, 343
Water play, 194, 218, 230, 273, 301,
   302, 304, 316, 342
"Way Up in the Sky So Blue," 123
Wheelbarrow game, 277
Wheeled toys, 363
"Where Is Baby?" 140
"Where Is Thumbkin?" 310
Wind chimes, 31
Wrapping paper, 300, 338
"Yankee Doodle," 172
Yoga, 96, 126
Zoo, 278

about gymboree

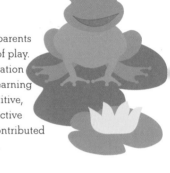

For more than a quarter century, Gymboree has helped parents and children discover the many pleasures and benefits of play. Based on established principles of early childhood education and administered by trained teachers, The Gymboree Learning Program emphasizes the wonder of play in a noncompetitive, nurturing environment. Gymboree, which runs its interactive parent-child programs in more than 29 countries, has contributed to the international awareness of the importance of play.

consulting editors

Dr. Roni Cohen Leiderman is a developmental psychologist specializing in emotional development, positive discipline, and play. For more than 25 years, she has worked with children, families, and professionals. She is associate dean of the Mailman Segal Institute for Early Childhood Studies at Nova Southeastern University in Fort Lauderdale, Florida, and the mother of two children.

Dr. Wendy Masi is a developmental psychologist specializing in early childhood. She has designed and implemented programs for preschools, families with young children, and early childhood professionals for more than 25 years. The mother of four children, Dr. Masi is dean of the Mailman Segal Institute for Early Childhood Studies at Nova Southeastern University.

author

Susan Elisabeth Davis, the mother of two children and an award-winning journalist, is the author of Gymboree's *Baby Play* and coauthor of Gymboree's *Toddler Play*.

illustrator

Christine Coirault, a children's book illustrator based in London, is the author of *The Little Book of Good Manners* and the illustrator of *How Do I Say That?*

photographer

Aaron Locke, owner of Aaron Locke Design & Photography, specializes in visual storytelling through graphic design and photography services.